ADVENTURE AND PROFIT IN THE WORLD'S BAZAARS

BY **CHRISTINA BLESSING**

LOST CITIES......LAS VEGAS, NEVADA

Adventure
and Profit
In the World's Bazaars

By Christina Blessing

Published by:

Lost Cities
3395 South Jones #204
Las Vegas, NV 89102 USA

Design, layout and editing by:

A𝗿t & Style
Post Office Box 5005
Rancho Santa Fe, CA 92067 USA

Library of Congress Catalog Number 95-79192
ISBN 0-9648194-8-1

Printed in the United States of America by Banta Book Group.

Table of Contents

Introduction

Adventure in the world's bazaars. Colorful characters. Exotic travel. More buying and selling opportunities than you could explore in a dozen lifetimes. Maybe a chance to get rich. Certainly many exciting alternatives to the daily 9 to 5.

Travel with a purpose. Financial and personal rewards can be substantial, but this kind of life and work is definitely not for everyone. By the time you finish reading this book you will have a pretty good idea whether or not it holds promise for you and, if so, how to get started.

Even if you do not choose to make this a full or part time business, you will profit by using the bargaining strategies in day to day situations. The travel planning hints can save you thousands of dollars and make your trips many times safer and more comfortable. You will learn how to take advantage of opportunities and avoid the traps that are so often lurking beneath the surface. Shipping and customs will seem less mysterious when you know how to deal with them.

Consider how the strategies relate to one another. As you formulate your plan try to look at things from different angles. Put yourself in the shoes of the buyers, sellers, and bureaucratic officials with whom you will be dealing. Do as much research as you can. Sort through the details. Get focused. Develop an implementation schedule. Then...

Chapter 1
A World of Treasures

Fabergé eggs at the Santa Fe flea market. Ancient Greek sculpture amongst a collection of arrowheads. An illuminated manuscript in a small shop on a Paris side street. Valuable rarities at garage sales. Passed over paintings by Raphael, Matisse, even Picasso hidden in rummage sale clutter. All for sale cheap. Such are the rumors of fabulous finds in the world's bazaars. Many of them are true. Making a once-in-a-lifetime discovery is not what this book is about. If you prowl around long enough you may come across something significant. However, most who successfully trade in these markets find their profits elsewhere.

Common utilitarian items discarded by one culture and elevated to collectible status by another offer the greatest opportunities. Prices can vary significantly from one region to another. These valuation differences are most often differences in taste or perception, but currency exchange rates and political factors also play a role.

Perhaps the best illustration of a recent exploitable situation of this type is the curious market in used blue jeans. This may prove to be as prophetic as it is illustrative since it casts the United States as the source of interesting tribal clothing rather than the market for it. In just about every city, town, and hamlet west of the Mississippi River there are signs offering to buy used blue jeans. Many bid up to $15 a pair for specific styles, or maybe even more. These offers certainly seem generous. Why is this happening? It seems that Japanese and Thai connoisseurs now consider these pieces of wearable Americana to be collectibles and are willing to pay $100, $500, $5,000, or more for an especially desirable specimen.

All the details are revealed in an intriguing article by Robert Sullivan in the April 1995 issue of *Vogue* magazine. It follows the trail from excursions by adventurous traders into the remote villages of America's West in search of the perfect jeans, to the wholesale marketplace of the once a month flea market at Los Angeles' Rose Bowl to the final consumer/collector in Asia.

Identifying discards to collectible situations is what much of this game is about. A meandering look at some other examples in the marketplace should inspire you to start thinking in a profitable direction.

Wearables and Other Textiles

American Indian weavings are a bit pricey to be considered undiscovered or undervalued, but Indian weavings from South and Central America may have possibilities. Many of them are of considerably better weaving quality than those from North America and almost all are substantially less expensive. Guatemala, Panama, Ecuador, Peru, and Bolivia all have interesting pieces. Oaxacan reproductions of American Indian designs are often nicer than the examples they are copying.

Southeast Asia offers Thai silks, hill tribe embroideries, and unusual selections from Burma, Laos, and Cambodia. You can find most of these at the Weekend Market in Bangkok or the Night Market in Chiang Mai.

China's ethnic diversity is represented by a cornucopia of woven delights from market cities like Kashgar in the wilds of Sinkiang province to Lhasa in Tibet to Beijing and Shanghai. Many floor coverings, symbolic wall hangings, and costumes are just beginning to show up in the western world.

Village and city workshop rugs as well as tribal flatweaves are found from the Himalayas through Central Asia to the Near East and Eastern Europe. The market for these has been weak recently, so there are bargains to be found.

American quilts are highly collectible in the U.S. and there are now international shows in Europe. How many masterpieces are hidden away in grannies' attics around the country?

The Saturday and Sunday markets in Buenos Aires and Montevideo have excellent selections of fine clothing from the early part of the twentieth century when Argentina and Uruguay were wealthier countries.

Jeans are not the only desirable vintage clothing available in the U.S. Leather jackets, old formal wear, and a changing array of odds and ends command premium prices from both domestic and international shoppers.

The Indian subcontinent has an abundance of workshop and tribal weavings. You can see them all in Delhi.

Examples from Africa range from the Berber rugs of Morocco to wearable indigo robes and the geometric designs of Kuba cloth in the sub-Saharan South. Kente cloth designs are currently produced in mass quantities, but the old ones still have collectible value.

Paintings and Frames

While you might stumble across an important painting, the chances of doing so are quite slim. However, there are other items in this realm that can be sold for a profit.

Any piece of art that you find in another country or even in distant regions of your own country is unfamiliar and exotic to local buyers. Some recent examples include black folk art of the Dixie South and Haiti and contemporary paintings from Russia, Vietnam, and China.

Old frames are almost always worth a look. Sometimes you can pick up really great ones for next to nothing. The Sunday San Telmo Fair in Buenos Aires had an outstanding selection the last time I visited there.

Furniture

Quality antique furniture is highly valued just about everywhere. Sometimes currency fluctuations can create opportunities for profit. This was true several years ago in Argentina. Nice nineteenth century pieces were available very cheap. Changes in the collective concept of furnishing style can also result in some bargains.

Antique reproductions from places like Thailand and Indonesia often look as good as the real thing and are much more durable. In Bangkok and Chiang Mai there are advertisements for old and new antiques. At least one company in South Africa is producing high quality primitive tables and decorative pieces made from old railroad ties and beams. The visual impact of these old exotic woods is impressive.

━━━━━━━━━━━━━━━━━━━━━━━

Unlike many South American cities, Montevideo does not have an enchanting colonial past. If you ask any of the locals about the beaches, they tell you to go to the one in Punta del Este. They say it is much better. There is a veterinary hospital that is open twenty-four hours a day.

On the streets leading away from Plaza Independencia are many small shops. You can buy dark, richly colored Uruguayan amethysts; coats made from the fur of seals, antelope, or unborn calf; early twentieth century art glass; and antiques.

I stopped in one shop that specialized in World War II memorabilia, but had a bit of everything. It was owned by a young expatriot Brit. The only piece that appealed to me was an old wooden table in the center of his showroom. He told me that it was a baker's table from one of the farmhouses in the countryside. I asked him if there were very many like it.

"In the nineteenth century, there were 50,000 farms in Uruguay. All of them had tables similar to this one. I don't know of anyone here besides me who thinks they are interesting."

Decorative Accessories

Decorative accessories represent one of the most fertile fields of exploration. When modern storage containers made of plastics and other space age materials came to India, out went the beautiful rosewood and mahogany bowls and boxes. Baskets, functional ceramics, and stoneware from many cultures have also been discarded over the years. You only need to figure out how to use them.

Jewelry

Many new importers have selected some type of jewelry as their initial product. It was a smart choice. In the past the quality of jewelry from foreign sources was better, there was more diversity, the materials were of higher quality, but most important it was CHEAP. This was true whether you selected from traditional local designs or commissioned production of your own design. It is still true in some countries, but the gap has narrowed. The quality of artist-made jewelry from the U.S. is already competitive and may become an interesting choice as an export item to both Europe and Asia.

Granulation and filigree seen on Balinese jewelry is accomplished by tedious, painstaking work. In the village of Celuk there are many small enclaves of silversmiths who specialize in this craft.

I bought thousands of pairs of plain and bejeweled earrings there, a hundred pieces at a time. The purchasing process was as tedious and painstaking as the creation of the jewelry. I frequently had to bargain for each individual style rather than buying the whole lot by weight. The financial result was the same for me. I weighed the prospective pieces and determined the appropriate price. The figure was no surprise to the vendor; the price I offered, and which was eventually accepted, was the market price for the village. Nevertheless, it was always necessary to go through the bargaining procedure.

After a particularly grueling session, my counterpart smiled and asked me if I liked animals. When I told him that I did, he invited me to look at collection. Not pets, collection. He and his younger brother led me back behind his house where there were exotic birds in cages and a morose monkey chained to a perch. He motioned me back toward what was becoming more swamp than backyard. We stopped in front of a large trough almost full of murky water.

"Do you want to see the snakes?", he asked as little brother fished around the trough with a hoe.

Several feet of thick snake began to appear, wrapped around the implement. The snake did not seem very energetic and allowed himself to be transferred to a nearby pen.

Little brother returned to searching the trough. After a short while, he began talking excitedly. Both of them looked concerned.

"He can't find the big one, but don't worry," he said reassuringly. "He's around here some-where."

The waist high weeds began to appear thicker. I could feel my shoes sinking into the mud. I started walking back toward the house.

"It's O.K. lady. Come back. Here he is in the pen."

I returned to see their python, a foot across and at least twelve feet long. They caught it nearby and were hoping to sell it.

Real Collectibles

Real collectibles are referred to as such because there is a recognized market for them, collector's organizations, shows, and publications. The possibility of good quality fake or reproduction pieces being represented as genuine is proportional to the level of interest in a particular realm. This does not mean that you should not involve yourself; it does mean that you need to acquire more than just a passing knowledge in order to be successful. Religious art, photographs, books, maps, antiquities, coins, paper money, antique and tribal jewelry, and weapons all fit into this category. Pieces that are cheap and look good won't get you into too much trouble, but make sure you know what you are doing before you spend important money. Remember what P.T. Barnum said.

This is far from being a comprehensive examination of what is available in the world's markets, but it should get you started. Buy things you like, not what you think other people will like. If you can work some of these possibilities into an existing business framework or use some special knowledge you already possess, so much the better your chances for success.

Chapter 2
Remarkable Markets

Where is the world's best market? A reasonable question but difficult to answer. What are you looking for? What are your language skills? What passport do you carry? Are you interested in price or quality? There are many complications. It can be productive to look at some examples of remarkable marketplaces and even more productive to visit them. You may begin to find some answers.

While several of the markets examined in this chapter are in what could be described as exotic locations, others are right here in the United States. In their own ways New York, Santa Fe, and Tucson stack up pretty well against Bangkok, Delhi, Marrakech, and Bali. Although none of these destinations qualify as new shopping discoveries they all offer memorable market experiences. They also present real opportunities for making money. If you want to make a trial run, any of these market cities are a good place to start.

New York City

The Statue of Liberty is the first sight for many new immigrants to the United States. New York is where they made their first home. In each group someone saw a need for something that was available in their old country and not readily available here. They started businesses based on those observations. Sometimes they were right, sometimes not. Their perception was often tested on the street. This is still true today.

Each weekend the streets of New York present an ever changing array of food, antique, junk, and treasure markets. Most of the best quality remains in Manhattan. Check out the area around West 25th Street and Sixth Avenue; Canal and Greene; Second Avenue near 56th Street; and Columbus Avenue and West 76th Street. Most of these markets have been around for awhile and will probably continue to be of interest. Look for other areas to explore. The Weekend section of the *New York Times* is your best source for new ideas.

While you will focus most of your attention on the street vendors, look at the curious little shops that populate these market areas. The competition keeps the prices from being much higher than on the street and you may find some real treasures.

You have ample opportunity to test all your marketplace skills in the street markets of New York City.

Santa Fe, New Mexico

To many people Santa Fe conjures up images of Georgia O'Keefe landscapes, adobe architecture, and turquoise jewelry, but few realize that this town of sixty plus thousand is one of the top three art markets in the United States. Lots and lots of money is spent there.

While Santa Fe is a year-round destination, for several weeks in August an extraordinary amount of top quality American Indian, Western, and antique ethnographic material from around the world is concentrated there. Many top dealers from around the country come there at this time to sell and to buy.

The best of the shows is the Antique Ethnographic Art Show and Sale which features antique tribal art, jewelry, and textiles from around the world. This show will give you a look at some of the quality pieces that are available in the world's marketplaces. You will also have a first hand look at prices which are usually somewhere between discounted retail and quantity wholesale.

The number of shows and auctions seems to increase each year. Check out as many of them as you can. Most are held at the Sweeney Convention Center or in hotel conference facilities near the plaza. The Santa Fe Chamber of Commerce can assist you with up to date information. Their phone number is 505-983-7317.

No shopping trip to Santa Fe would be complete without a stop at Trader Jack's Flea Market. Located just past the Santa Fe Opera on the road to Taos, this market has become famous from word of mouth raves, articles in New York and Chicago newspapers, and other publicity. Everyone from movie stars to desert lowlife shop there. Since it only costs ten dollars or so per day for space, the range in merchandise is quite varied. Some of the vendors at the top Santa Fe shows set up there. There is also a certain amount of garage sale junk. Parking is a problem at times and there seems to have been a bit of a decline in the overall quality of merchandise, but this is still a great place to buy and sell.

Tucson, Arizona

Tucson might seem like an unusual location for the largest gem show in the country, but that is exactly what it becomes the first couple of weeks each February. More than twenty retail, wholesale, and semi-wholesale shows are held in venues ranging from the convention center to both premium and marginal hotels to a gas station to booths set up along the side of the road.

The Tucson experience is not for everyone. One first time attendee (a genteel southern belle who is involved with the promotion of upscale craft shows) commented that her most vivid memories were of "Africans laying under the trees with their beads, far too many places where a lady had to walk through the gravel with her good shoes on, and rats in the pool.

All this notwithstanding, Tucson in February is an important marketplace and attracts buyers and exhibitors from around the world. Millions of dollars change hands on fine colored gemstones, beads, mineral specimens, fossils, and jewelry. If you are interested in any of these areas you need to go there at least once.

Verification of wholesale credentials varies from show to show but is usually fairly strict at the quality locations. You need a copy of your business license and/or sales tax permit. Contact the show promoters directly for buyer registration and other specific information. A few of the best are listed as follows:

Gem and Lapidary Wholesalers
601-879-8832
Shows at: Holiday Inn-Holidome
4550 Palo Verde Blvd.

Rodeway Inn
I-10@Grant Road

Arizona Mineral and Fossil Show
303-674-2713
Shows at: Best Western Executive Inn
              333 W. Drachman

              Quality Inn
              1601 N. Oracle

American Gem Trade Association
800-972-1162
Show at: Tucson Convention Center
              260 S. Church Street

Gem and Lapidary Dealers Association
602-742-5455
Show at: Holiday Inn-Broadway
              (City Center)
              181 W. Broadway

Atrium Productions
602-998-4000
Show at: Pueblo Inn
              350 S. Freeway

This is a good cross section of what is available, but by no means complete. New shows are added almost every year and some fade away. *Colored Stone* magazine publishes a comprehensive show guide each year that is essential for the first time and experienced participant alike. Their subscription customer service number is 610-293-0564. An associated publication, *Lapidary Journal*, also provides show information.

Bangkok, Thailand

In many respects Bangkok is the ideal initial foreign market to explore. It has good hotels, food and business services; travel arrangements are relatively simple; many people speak English; there are few currency regulations; the customs procedure is relatively uncomplicated; reliable shippers are readily available. In addition, there are many truly wholesale colored gem dealers, a multitude of antique dealers with shops chock full of interesting fare from Thailand and other countries of the region, and the massive Weekend Market.

The Weekend Market is held every Saturday and Sunday in Chatuchak Park. Just say the words Weekend Market (on the appropriate days, of course) and you will be transported to one of the largest traditional markets in Asia. Over the years the market has gotten cleaner and more organized. Some stalls are now air conditioned. Correspondingly, prices have crept up on the quality antiques. Still, there is a great selection of textiles, jewelry, utilitarian items, and weapons from Thailand, Burma, Cambodia, Laos, and China. And for free, an unforgettable sampling of the market experience.

There is much fertile ground in Bangkok for application of the techniques discussed in future chapters. The guide book, Shopping in Exotic Thailand, by Ronald Krannich and Caryl Rae Krannich can provide you with some ideas about where to start.

Delhi, India

The area around the Red Fort and continuing west through the Chandi Chowk bazaar offers the finest antique tribal and ethnographic shopping in India. Look past the tourist junk and into the shops, both downstairs and upstairs. Do not ignore the narrow lanes and passageways. This area offers not only discoveries from India's multicultural past, but also those from other countries in the region including Nepal, Tibet, Pakistan, Bhutan, and

Afghanistan, as well as tribal protectorates such as Mizzoram, Assam, and Sikkim.

Most maps in the guide books will get you headed in the right direction. Make sure not to take any recommendations of specific shops too seriously. Wander around purposefully and you will do just fine.

Marrakech, Morocco

There is no place in the world like the Djemaa al Fna, the main square in Marrakech's old walled city. Complete with snake charmers, storytellers, food vendors, clowns, acrobats, pickpockets, weary semi-trained animals, child boxers, and a raggedy assortment of street hustlers, this center of activity is experienced more as a sense of immersion in otherness rather than a mere observation. I doubt that the feel of the place or the characters are much different than they were centuries ago.

Heading north from the Djemaa al Fna are the labyrinth of souks. This was a major stop on the centuries old North African caravan routes and is still a trading center today. There are contemporary trinkets and handicrafts and occasionally, some old Berber rugs, tribal silver and jewelry, and other antiques including weapons. To be commercially successful in this market you need to spend more than the usual amount of time searching for the right contacts. Avoiding the touts can be almost impossible, but it can be done. For most visitors, the experience is the real treasure.

Bali, Indonesia

The island of Bali, off the eastern edge of Java is the perfect destination for those looking for fun, sun, and relaxation along with their marketplace activities. Great food, comfortable accommodations, volcanos, white sand beaches, picturesque villages, and an abundance of first rate handicrafts and interesting antiques make it an excellent choice.

Handicrafts include carved wooden masks and figures, granulated and filagree gold and silver jewelry, stonecarvings, and magnificent textiles from throughout Indonesia. Antique furniture and boxes, ceramics, beads, puppets, textiles, and more await your discovery. Rent a car to avoid the high commission touts and guides and allow yourself time to explore the island. <u>Shopping and Traveling in Exotic Indonesia</u> by Ronald Krannich and Caryl Rae Krannich has a lot of useful information, especially about the individual villages.

All of these remarkable markets have qualities that have made lasting impressions on me. They also offer valuable experiences for anyone beginning an international bazaar adventure. BUT!!! None of these places will necessarily be the best one for you. Only research, exploration, and traveling through the maze of obstacles and opportunities will lead to your ideal marketplace. There are suggestions to help you find the best market in any city in Chapter 8, In The Market.

Chapter 3
Communicate Anywhere

Communication involves the exchange of ideas and opinions, the expression of desires and emotions. You must develop competence in getting your message across without full use of your normal cues and tools. Systematic planning and study can take away a lot of the uncertainty. Observation and patience can help you to latch onto nonverbal patterns and actions that transcend the spoken word.

Communication in strange and exotic lands can be both easier and more difficult than you expect. For example, almost anyone you need to interact with in Thailand (other than taxi drivers) speaks English while almost no one in Argentina does.

Before examining strategies and shortcuts, make sure you use the skills that you already possess to best advantage. It is even more important to make sure that you do not misuse them.

Speaking English

That you speak English fluently is a communication skill of enormous magnitude. Unless you have traveled a great deal, you may not truly appreciate its significance. It gives you a giant head start over those who only speak Spanish, French, Japanese, Chinese... anything else. English is the international language of business and you speak it.

Always try to communicate in English before resorting to other options. It is most likely your vehicle of common understanding. Besides, even if you speak the other language, you do not speak or understand it as well as you think. This is especially if your only exposure to it was high school or college study. In some countries the locals may understand English as well as your broken attempts at their language, yet refuse to acknowledge comprehending either. More often the people you meet do what they can to enable both of you to be understood.

As part of my preparation for a trip to Morocco, I took a four week, eight hour per day intensive course in French. I did not expect to become fluent in that short amount of time, but I thought the course coupled with my year of high school French would enable me to get by. (I did not even consider trying to learn Arabic. It may have been more appropriate, but it seemed impossible at the time.)

My Air Maroc flight from New York made three attempts to land at the airport in Casablanca in heavy fog. Each time the landing was aborted with a steep, stomach-churning climb. Finally the stewardess announced that we would detour to Marrakech where we would wait on the ground until the fog cleared. My final destination was Marrakech, but because my original flight was scheduled to land in Casablanca, that is where I had to deplane.

After a four hour wait on the runway in Marrakech my flight returned to Casablanca. Customs was a breeze. I made my way to the Air Maroc ticket counter. My scheduled flight to Marrakech left an hour before. Another one was leaving in about thirty minutes and I needed a seat.

Speaking slowly and carefully in French, I explained my problem first to one ticket agent then to another. I may as well have been speaking Martian. They seemed to have no idea what I was talking about while I understood most of what they were saying. I tried to switch to English. There was no communication breakthrough. They continued to talk about me but not to me. One of the agents led me to a seat in the corner and and motioned for me to sit there. After everyone in line had boarded the plane, a different agent approached me and handed me a boarding pass and told me in English to hurry.

At first, I couldn't decide if my treatment was due to my terrible French or if it was standard for stand-by passengers on Air Maroc. I had no trouble being understood on the remainder of my Moroccan trip and I had no difficulties on future Air Maroc Flights. I'm pretty sure I was a victim of language snobbery.

Try to recognize which English words your conversation mate understands. Make a special effort to use them. You do not need a very large mutual vocabulary to exchange significant amounts of information.

Use simple words. Consider the words you use as a reverse grid of the words you would have learned if you studied his language.

The Ugly American

Do not turn communication efforts into a disadvantage. Do not raise your voice unless you have a compelling reason for doing so. The only time that aggressive behavior may be appropriate is when there is something serious that you want changed immediately. Only consider this after you have tried to get your point across politely. Even then it should be an act of sorts. You are trying to change the tempo. As soon as you regain some control return to a polite and firm posture.

Most of the world's inhabitants have pretty good feelings toward Americans. Why this is true I am not certain. They see us as being rather strange and unpredictable, but on the whole they actually seem to like us. Given some of the U.S. foreign policy misadventures of the past few decades and the imperious way in which some of us act when abroad, I find this nothing less than remarkable. Sometimes I think that the most positive thing that can be said about Americans traveling overseas is that we are not as obnoxious as others.

Do your best to stay relaxed when trying to get your point across. Do not act officious or self important. It can be easy to get irritated with perceived inefficiency. Be friendly. Be businesslike. If there is a problem try to make it our problem, not my problem or your problem. Find different ways to ask "What can we do to take care of this?" Using a firm, friendly, neutral tone can keep you at the top of the problem solving pile. Getting visibly angry can result in sudden cases of "No speaka English" or worse.

Foreign Languages

English is understood at most travel agencies, hotels, government offices, and shippers. Taxi drivers, waiters, and near-to-the-source merchants are frequently a different story. To function successfully in the marketplace, you have to develop some capabilities with local languages.

Prior training in the local language can be a mixed blessing. You will probably tend to overestimate your proficiency. Unless this language is your second tongue or unless you have truly superior linguistic talents, you will conclude that you do not speak it at all after a few non-classroom experiences. Most people have a difficult time effectively expressing themselves in multiple languages if they do not speak them regularly in day-to-day settings and situations. There are also dialects and idiomatic expressions to be dealt with. The best carryover from your previous study will be familiarity with how the language sounds.

Books, Tapes, and the Script

Language books and tapes offer limited benefits in developing communications skills. Most offer a jumble of too much material to learn effectively in a short period of preparation. By trying to learn too much you will learn nothing.

A practical solution to this is to develop your own carefully scripted scenes. Then work on finding the appropriate foreign phrases. Here the books and tapes can be useful. The best combination is for the book to have phonetic pronunciations which you can hear by listening to the tapes. These book/tape packages are often sealed so you can't see what you are getting. They range in quality from excellent to awful. Barron's "Getting By" series is a good choice. All of them seem to have useful phrase selections and comprehensive tapes.

The useful phrases selected by the language study packagers are often not the ones which you would choose. For example, the dating section in one Arabic language course could lead to some fairly unpleasant consequences for the unsuspecting non-Arabic male. It is sometimes better not to know how to say what you are thinking.

Barron's Educational Services, Inc. puts out an excellent, but fairly expensive comprehensive package. Several years ago the list price was $75 for their Spanish course. It contained a 600+ page book with phonetic pronunciations of the dialogues along with twelve tapes which corresponded to pages in the book. If you want to take six months to really learn a language, this is the ticket. This course was developed for the Department of State's Foreign Service Institute. It focuses on common, everyday situations. It teaches recurring patterns. The dialogues use the words that people actually say. You can reach them at:

Barron's Educational Services
250 Wireless Boulevard Road
Hauppage, NY 11788

Complete your script prior to selecting the books and tapes. It will take several hours to do this.

The structure that you use in constructing your script will differ from that of a normal dialogue. Since you do not know nearly enough to become involved in a real conversation, concentrate on making your wishes known. Determine the things you want and how to ask for them. These include food and drink, transportation, and the items you want to purchase. You are only interested in expressing your wishes and determining whether or not they will be fulfilled. This is what I want. Is the answer yes or no? This is not as effective as a two-sided interchange, but it does have one offsetting advantage. You are not geared to understanding explanations or excuses. Consequently, you may not have listen to as many.

The following sample script was used on my last trip to Brazil. It is fairly extensive due to some carryover between Portuguese and my passing capabilities in Spanish.

Script

Transportation

Take me to the airport
Hotel Gloria
this address
Stop here
Can you wait?
I will return in ten minutes

Pleasantries and Essentials

yes
no
where
when
how
which
this
that
for
to
in
and
good day
good night
Do you speak English?
I do not speak Portuguese
thank you
excuse me
please

Descriptions

large
small

hot
cold
old
new
final
good
bad
expensive
cheap
more
less
my
your

Action

to understand
I understand
you understand
to eat
I eat
you eat
to have
I have
you have
to be
I am
you are
to want
I want
you want
to be able
I am able
you are able
to leave
I leave
you leave
to return

I return
you return
to go
I go
you go
to buy
I buy
you buy
to sell
I sell
you sell

Colors

black
white
red
yellow
blue
green

Numbers

1-20 (by ones)
30-90 (by tens)
hundred
thousand
million

Shopping

How much?
ring
gem
gold
earrings
bracelet
carats

Food and Drink

mineral water (not carbonated)
coffee
tea
orange juice
red wine
beer
rice
potatoes
vegetables
chicken
lobster
shrimp
the bill

Changing Money

I want to change dollars
What is the exchange rate?
bank

Look over the sample. Pay particular attention to how the sections interrelate. The object is to be able to convey the information which is most important to you. You want to be understood. Grammar is of very little importance. The only part of verb conjugations are I and you, for example. Plurals are ignored.

Do not simply copy the master phrases suggested in the sample. They are points of departure. Take time to personalize it. Identify your key words. Consider how familiar you are with the language and how difficult it is for you. The easier it is for you, the more words, phrases and patterns you can add. Most Westerners feel more comfortable with the Romance languages than with ones such as Arabic, Thai, or Tibetan.

Relax somewhere quietly and visualize the situations you might encounter. Identify the critical details. How can you get your point across most concisely? Take notes. Go from event to event. Try to cover as much territory as you can. Compare your notes for the critical areas of the various situations. Common situations as well as your key words are the ones you want to learn. Also make sure that you can recognize the expected replies to your requests. Phrase the requests in such a way that the number of possible responses are as few and as narrow as possible.

You should be comfortable with your group of words and phrases within twenty days if you practice an hour per day. Do not try to condense it into a fewer number of longer sessions. Repetition over time is most important. Keep your list with you. Practice it on the plane on the way over. Practice it in the morning before you go out.

Chapter 4
Professional Travel Planning

When you plan travel with business objectives, your concerns and focus are different than when you travel for fun and frolic. This is especially true if your business involves import and export. The choices for transportation and accommodations will be more complicated. Security, availability of business services, non-stop flights, and variations in customs procedures at different points of entry and departure will become more important.

You need to contact foreign embassies, consulates, and foreign shippers to prepare for dealing with red tape. There may also be some questions for U.S. Customs or Fish and Wildlife.

Plans and preparations require your direct involvement. This involves tedious research and telephone work, but it must be done. The time you spend on planning and organization is leveraged throughout your entire trip and is responsible for its success or failure. It would be impossible to emphasize this too strongly.

Travel planning can be broken down in a variety of ways. The following divisions follow a logical order. It does not make much sense, for example, to buy your airline tickets before you find out about the entry requirements to your destination.

Destination Research
Foreign Import/Export Requirements
U.S. Customs Requirements
   Documents
   Transportation

Accommodations
Daily Plan
Money
Packing
Notifications and Backups

You will not have all green lights every step of the way. The dreaded grey area pops up all too often in travel and import/export related areas. Try to get specific answers to your questions. Pin people down. Accumulate as much information as you can. Make your best educated decision. Resign yourself to the fact that you will make some mistakes. Hope that they are not devastating ones and don't let the obstacles discourage you too much.

Destination Research

Travel books are the best resource for exploring the lay of foreign lands from the safety and comfort of your couch. They give you insights into local behavior, holidays, markets, hotel and airline possibilities, restaurants, and maps. You may find some potential purchasing ideas also, but beware of suggested places of purchase. You will get information about the official line on entry requirements, currency regulations, and possible export problems at the time the book was written.

The sections on local customs and history are at the beginning of most travel books. Here you can find out about attitudes toward Americans, special courtesies or expectations, and unusual faux pas that might mark you as ill-bred.

Holiday information can also be very important. Most prospective Western travelers to Islamic countries are warned against going to these destinations during Ramadan, but other festivities can interfere with your plans as well. For example, many businesses shut down for up to a week during Chinese New Year... something that you might not have expected.

Locations of major markets, the days and times of operation, and the types of goods sold are useful facts that are provided by good travel guides. Some travel books give you the feel of the market also if you read between the lines. Even if the market is not particularly recommended by the book try to check it out if at all possible. One travel guide, that was in many other ways quite useful, disparaged the Weekend Market in Bangkok as having little of interest for the serious shopper. While that may have been true at the time the book was written, by the time it was released it offered the best selection of antiques in Thailand... much better than those offered in Chiang Mai's night market, which it had recommended. The author, who seemed knowledgeable, had probably not made a mistake. Times had changed.

Hotel recommendations given by travel books are usually pretty good. Make a note of those that appear to fit your needs. Suggestions from travel agents are spotty... some excellent, but others pretty awful.

You can also check the listings in Hotel & Travel Index, a quarterly directory of hotels and motels throughout the world. This hefty tome is thicker than a dictionary and weighs in at 15 pounds or so. Its listings of over 45,000 hotel, motel, and resorts worldwide give you potential places to stay just about anywhere. The maps of hotel locations are especially helpful. The commercial ads offer fairly comprehensive, although obviously biased information covering facilities and services. A copy from Summer 1990 is still a very useful planning tool for me. A friendly travel agency may be willing to allow you to browse through their latest issue or it may be in stock at a major library. If you are planning to travel extensively, you can order your own copy by contacting Hotel & Travel Index by phone at 201-902-2000, fax at 201-319-1628, or by mail at:

Hotel & Travel Index
500 Plaza Drive
Secaucus, NJ 07096

You can usually trust guidebook restaurant recommendations. Prices in their favored dining establishments are a bit higher priced than you might find elsewhere but the food quality makes up for it. Note the places that look interesting or are in the vicinity of where you expect to be spending a lot of time. You probably will not eat all of your meals in guidebook restaurants, but it does help to have something in mind when you find yourself getting hungry. Pay attention to the hours of operation. They are often different from the eating times that are normal for you. You do not want to find that your choice has just shut down for the next four or five hours when you are really starving.

Detailed maps of shopping and market areas are of primary importance. Always buy the book with the best maps. If you need more information, buy a second guide as well.

Be wary of specific shopping recommendations. It is tempting to tell you to never set foot inside any recommended shop. Some guidebook authors who recognize the problems of specific suggestions now only describe general shopping and market areas. This information is very useful and makes these books worth buying. List street names or regions that look promising and mark them on your map. If many of them are near each other, try to stay as close to that area as possible.

Entry requirements, import/export information, currency considerations, and other official policy information given by travel guides should be verified by contacting the appropriate foreign embassies or consulates before you make actual travel arrangements. Preliminary information can alert you to situations that make it impossible to conduct the type of business you are planning. This keeps you from wasting time or money on projects with no possible way of succeeding due to bureaucratic obstacles.

Be aware of changes in rules and regulations that create opportunities in previously inaccessible areas. Read as many periodicals as you can that are associated with your realm of interest as well as those associated with international business and trade. *Asia Week* and *The Economist* are good magazines to keep you up to date on perils and opportunities.

Selecting the best travel guidebook is a very personal decision. It involves not only your objectives but also your philosophy of travel. What is one person's ideal reference will be virtually useless to another. With that in mind, here are the ones that make my short list: Fodor's, Lonely Planet, and Impact Publications.

Fodor's family of travel books offers the best in mainstream travel information for most primary worldwide destinations and a few that are off the beaten path. Hotel and restaurant recommendations are divided by price ranges and are usually on the money. The annual "Highlights" and "Fodor's Choice" at the beginning of each guide should not be overlooked. If your destination is covered you cannot go wrong consulting Fodor's. They are available in almost any bookstore or you can reach them directly at:

Fodor's Travel Publications
201 East 50th Street
New York, NY 10022

Although they are now beginning to cover Europe and other somewhat civilized areas, Lonely Planet has long been the premier adventure travel guide publisher. They were often not only the best guide to the hinterlands, they were the only guide. An unwashed 60s feel seems to permeate, and many would be well advised to avoid their lower and middle priced accommodation suggestions. Nonetheless, the unparalleled map selection and many practical travel hints (especially on dealing with red tape) make this group of guidebooks valuable additions to any traveler's library. They also enjoy wide distribution or can be contacted in the U.S. at:

Lonely Planet Publications
PO Box 2001A
Berkeley, CA 94702

Impact Publications offers some unique insights into travel and shopping in Indonesia, Thailand, Hong Kong, and Singapore, among other places. Most of their books have been titled <u>Shopping in Exotic...</u>, <u>Traveling and Shopping in Exotic...</u>, or some similar form. Look for them in the bookstores. You can contact them at:

Impact Publications
10655 Big Oak Circle
Manassas, VA 22111-3040

The United States Department of State's Consular Information sheets give current, sometimes otherwise unavailable reports of unusual regulations or situations that may effect travelers. They also provide addresses and emergency phone numbers for U.S. consulates and embassies. If the State Department feels that conditions are particularly dangerous they issue a travel warning. While these warnings may not be sufficient reason to cancel or delay a trip, consider them along with the rest of your information. If you have real doubts about the viability of your trip, try to contact the U.S. consulate or embassy directly in your target country. Their number is available in your guidebook or in the consular report.

The information sheets and travel warnings are available at any of the regional passport agencies, at overseas U.S.

embassies and consulates, or by sending a self-addressed, stamped envelope to:

Overseas Citizens Services
Room 4811
Department of State
Washington, D.C. 20520-4818

You can also get both the information sheets and travel warnings 24 hours a day by telephone, fax, or modem. To access by touchtone phone call 202-647-5225. To receive them by fax call 202-647-3000 and follow the prompts. To view or download by computer call 202-647-9225 and set your software to N-8-1. The information is free other than regular long distance charges.

Go over your notes and think about the viability of your project in your target countries. If it looks good, you are ready to go on to the next task of confirming the details regarding foreign import/export requirements. If not, it's back to the drawing board to consider variations of your project that are currently possible. Perhaps you will have to look at alternative countries that are more accommodating.

Foreign Import/Export Requirements

The most difficult part of this very critical segment is to get facts that apply to your situation. This is often almost impossible to do in a positive sense. Even if you are assured by the U.S. branch of the embassy or consulate that what you want to do is okay, you may still run into problems overseas. In other countries they will probably not care very much what you were told here. Even if you have something in writing, you have no assurances that it will be considered valid. Consult Chapter 10, Getting It Safely Home, for additional thoughts on this subject. Try to get a feel for what the policies appear to be. Generally, you should forget about those situations where you are met with open hostility.

Cautiously explore the others. If you decide to go through with your project, risk as little as possible until you feel comfortable with the procedure.

The best information is uncovered if you are able to establish personal rapport with someone at the embassy or consulate. For this purpose consulates are usually the better choice. While embassies deal with the important official matters of state, consulates are on occasion honorary offices given to raise the status of those who are politically connected. These folks have little in the way of official responsibilities. They often seem to be delighted to chat with someone interested in traveling to their country. While they can be veritable warehouses of information, specific business contacts suggested by them, other than potential shippers, have never proven valuable to me. The answers you receive at a consulate are usually more straightforward than than the ones given by the staff at the embassy. Go visit in person if possible.

Shippers and freight forwarders in your target country can be outstanding sources of information if you can connect with them. Recommendations from foreign chambers of commerce, consulates, or embassies will be your best bets for locating them from the U.S. Communicate your request by fax if possible. Someone in their offices should be able to communicate in English, but you may not reach that person if you telephone. Be specific about the exact types of merchandise you want to export. If the items are antique be sure to include that information. Now is the time to find out about any problems you can expect. After you make your purchases it is usually too late.

U.S. Customs Requirements

U.S. Customs regulations are much more straightforward than those you will encounter in your foreign undertakings. The best information is available from the customs broker you select or from the U.S. Customs specialist for the type of merchandise you want to import. Contact Fish and Wildlife if animal products are involved. Appendix 3 lists contact numbers for U.S. Customs, Fish and Wildlife, and possible customs brokers in several gateway cities. If you supply accurate descriptions of what you are planning to do, you should receive accurate answers as to legality and special requirements.

Travel Documents

Passports

Your passport is the most important travel document. Without one your travel possibilities are limited. Make certain that your passport has at least six months remaining until expiration at the end of your trip. If not, get a replacement. Some countries do not recognize those with less time remaining as valid. If you do not have a passport get one now. Appendix 1 has all the gory details.

Guard your passport as you would any valuable... both here and abroad. If it is lost or stolen you are in for a frustrating, time-consuming experience.

Foreign Entry and Exit Requirements

First determine if you need an entry visa, and if so, how to get it. Also find out about immunizations; exit documents; departure taxes (determine if they are to be paid in local currency and, if so, make a note to have that amount set aside); currency restrictions and reporting requirements, both for entry and exit.

At the end of your inquiry ask, "Is there anything else that I should know about?" The staff at the embassies and consulates may be able to suggest ways around some of your thorniest problems. Ask for their advice. If there is anything you do not understand, keep asking questions until it is clear to you.

Allow plenty of time to arrange for your visas. Two weeks for each is a good guideline. Since you are sending your passport back and forth, always use a courier service such as Federal Express or UPS to transmit your package. Find out from each of the embassies how to arrange prepayment to have it shipped back to you by courier service also. Some have rather strict requirements for this.

Telephone numbers for the embassies of most countries are given in Appendix 2. Consulates are given by state when available. For countries that are not included, try directory assistance in Washington, D.C. or New York City. You can also order a copy of *Foreign Entry Requirements* which is compiled by the U.S. Department of State. The current price is fifty cents. Send your request to:

Consumer Information Center
Pueblo, CO 81009

Although this publication is updated annually, verify the information with the appropriate embassy or consulate.

Transportation

Airlines

There are several ways to make your airline travel arrangements. Each has pluses and minuses.

First, you can make them on your own by contacting the airline directly. To get the airlines toll free number call 1-800-555-1212 and request it. You can get flight information (days of the week, times, etc.) from the airline to aid in your preliminary preparation. When it is time to make your reservations, this is not usually the most convenient or economical method. While the rates quoted by the reservations agents of international airlines are usually less confusing than those given by their domestic counterparts, it is unlikely that you will ever encounter a true bargain.

You can access flight and time information on an increasingly complete basis by computer modem. Eventually, perhaps even now if you know where to look, you will be able to make discount travel arrangements this way.

If you are not a seasoned traveler or if you want travel recommendations, an experienced full service travel agent can be useful. If the agent has traveled to your destination and is familiar with your requirements, you can get some valuable advice. You may also be able to book a combination air/hotel package that saves money.

However, unless you really need lots of guidance and hand holding, a discount travel agent can usually do everything you need to have done...and cheaper. The best place to find one is in your local Sunday newspaper or that of the proposed gateway city. Look at the travel section and call several of the travel agents who have cheap flights to your destination. Try to get non-stop flights with reasonable departure and arrival times on carriers you know and like. (A direct flight is not a non-stop flight. You do not change planes, but the one you are on will make at least one stop. Direct flights can be okay and are sometimes the only way to get where you want to go. If the price is close, reserve non-stop if you can.) Try to avoid plane changes, long layovers, and airlines that are unfamiliar or make you feel uncomfortable. Since you will very seldom find exactly what you want, consider the trade-offs and make your best choice. To be on the safe side, check last year's phone book to see if your chosen discounter was in business then. A call to the Better Business Bureau that could uncover a history of unresolved complaints probably wouldn't hurt either. In case you were wondering how they can sell cheaper than regular travel agents, the simple answer is that they make a commitment to a particular air carrier for a large number of seats each month or quarter for a discounted price. They then need to sell them. You can save 20% or more off your ticket. Sometimes you can get a bigger discount if you pay cash than if you pay by credit card. Ask.

CHECK your ticket very closely against your itinerary before you pay for it. Changes or cancellations after you have been ticketed can be difficult and expensive. They may be impossible after the ticket has been issued. (You will find that changes you need to make after the first leg of the trip has been completed can be accomplished more easily... sometimes with no problems at all. It varies from airline to airline.)

LOOK at the status box for each line of your destinations. For you to have a confirmed seat it must read "OK". Anything else is unacceptable. Do not let anyone tell you that it is just fine to be at the top of the waiting list, that everything will be alright. It may be or it may not be. You want every seat confirmed on every segment of your flights, both going and coming, before you pay for the ticket. If you fail to do this you will find that no amount of weeping and gnashing of teeth after it has become a problem will help. You will be stuck... for how long is anybody's guess.

RECONFIRM all international flights 72 hours before they are scheduled to depart. Failure to do so can result in you being bumped with no compensation. They might not even want to listen sympathetically to your tale of woe. If you do this by phone try to get a reconfirmation number. (This is often not possible.) The best way is to go directly to an office of the airline. If you reconfirm there, they will not only enter this information into their computer, but will also make a nice official-looking mark on your ticket. How much weight this mark carries is uncertain, but it always makes me feel more secure.

If you travel by air on a regular basis The Airline Passenger's Guerrilla Handbook (ISBN 0-924022-04-3) by George Albert Brown provides advice that is indispensible, both on the plane and in and around airports. It discusses in detail almost everything about flying on commercial flights. Included are tried and proven techniques for coping with common frustrations; rules and regulations and how to bend them to your advantage; fear of flying and what to do about it; airline clubs; consumer air travel newsletters; and so on. It's worth the money.

Ground Transportation

You need to decide whether to take taxis, ride on public transportation, hire a car and driver, or rent a car and drive it yourself. In general, it is best not to drive in unfamiliar places. Plan to use the other transportation alternatives with the thought that you will drive yourself only in special circumstances. The Transportation section of Chapter 7 has suggestions for dealing with the local rules of the road, handling drivers, and avoiding difficulties.

If you are considering renting a car, find out if it is cheaper to make reservations here or at your destination. If you make arrangements before you leave, you may be required to pay in advance in exchange for a voucher. Your payment will probably be non-refundable. Consult your guidebook and the U.S. headquarters of major car rental companies.

If you need to have an international driver's license to rent a car, you can obtain one through automobile/insurance organizations such as AAA. A current driver's license, two passport sized photos, and a fee of about $10 are required. The picture identification you receive is valid for one year and represents in numerous languages that you are licensed to drive in your country of residence.

Accommodations

Location, security, price, and business service availability should all be evaluated when choosing where to stay. Check the guidebooks and the Hotel & Travel Index if you have access to one. Consider their suggestions along with any recommendations you have received and make your best choice.

You can reserve directly or through your full service or discount travel agent. If you are doing it yourself, send the request for reservations by fax and ask for their commercial rate. A credit card is required to guarantee the room so include the number, type, and expiration date. Leave a fax number for them to send confirmation.

A travel agent who makes your hotel reservations will collect the full amount in advance and issue you a voucher. Make a copy of it and keep it safe with the rest of your travel documents. Most of the time this works just fine. Unfortunately disagreements do arise about exactly what is covered. Have your agent supply you with a written summary of that information. This will not help you at the hotel if there is a misunderstanding, but it may help you to recover something from the agent in the aftermath. Get the hotel to give you a written statement of any discrepancy as well as a copy of the bill.

Daily Plan

The daily plan/itinerary is a systematic method of organizing your priorities and activities for each day of your trip. Putting it together is probably the greatest benefit as it forces you to consider your goals and how to accomplish them. You will leverage the time you spend on planning throughout your trip. Design your daily plan to your best advantage. One simple effective style is shown below.

City, Country

Wake-up Call (Time)_____

Morning Activities

Afternoon Activities

Evening Activities

Special "Tools for the Day"

Transportation

Priority Tasks
(Reconfirmations, etc.)

Group these together in a binder or folder and review them before you go to bed each evening. It is a good way to evaluate your progress on a daily basis. If you are covering ground quickly, you can add on some of your optional ventures. If things are going slowly, you may have some rearranging to do.

Money

Currency Declaration

If you are withdrawing a large sum of cash from your bank, let them know about it several days in advance. Try to get new bills since overseas merchants may be reluctant to accept torn or ratty ones.

If the amount withdrawn is more than $10,000 or if the teller is feeling overly vigilant, you will be asked to provide information for Department of Treasury Form 4789, a Currency Transaction Report. Have them make a copy for you and keep it with your travel documents. This shows where the money came from if you are questioned about it. There are some very interesting laws on the books that allow your cash to be arrested and taken from you if the authorities believe you got it under suspicious circumstances. This documentation does not completely protect you but it does show that you are trying to do things the way they seem to want them done.

If you have $10,000 or more in cash or negotiable instruments when you leave the country, locate the U.S. Customs office in the airport after you check in for your flight. Tell them you want to fill out a currency declaration form. This will avoid unpleasantness if there is a customs search or if you have to explain how you paid for everything when you return.

When you return to the United States you need to make a declaration if you have more than $10,000. You can use the customs form that you are given on the plane before arriving to make that declaration.

Complying with these regulations may seem to be a waste of time. They may seem intrusive. Following them to the letter is another part of properly preparing for your trip. If you ignore them you allow another possibility for disaster to creep into the picture. Non-compliance is not a problem unless it is. Then it is serious.

Travelers' Checks

You may want to consider travelers' checks if you are certain they will be acceptable for your use and if you are nervous about carrying a lot of cash. Those issued by American Express, MasterCard, and Visa have the widest acceptance. Check with the issuer or your guidebook about how to redeem them at your destination. Shop around and check with any organizations you belong to for discounted or waived rates. AAA has had them available for no additional charge over face value. There may be restrictions on the amounts you can purchase at these premium free rates.

Credit Cards

You will not usually be able to use a credit card to purchase merchandise at the most favorable terms. You may want to carry one to pay for hotel and other travel expenses or for emergencies. Know what your limit is before you leave and do not exceed it while you are abroad. Although it has not happened frequently, American travelers have been detained by police after a charge made by them was subsequently refused because they were over their limit. A debit card attached to a money market fund has the advantage of allowing you to set your own spending limits based on the amount you have in your account at the time. These are available through cash management accounts offered by major brokerage companies. They are gradually becoming available through banks.

Packing

Pack sparsely and take extra money is the best advice for overseas travel. There may be some things that are essential to you that are not be readily available at your destination. Determine what they are and bring them. Carefully read Chapter 5, The Shopping Kit and Other Things You Will be Glad You Brought. Pack early. A day or two in advance is not too far ahead. This gives you time to figure out if you remembered everything.

A Word of WARNING. Everyone is aware by now of the dangers of having anything to do with illegal drugs in foreign countries. There should be no need to recount tales of the unpleasant fates of those unfortunates so involved. Even if you would never intentionally run afoul of these laws there are precautions that you should take to avoid becoming inadvertently entangled.

If you bring prescription drugs with you, leave them in their original container and carry a copy of your prescription. This is especially important if the drugs are of the type that have any potential for abuse, such as tranquilizers.

Do not bring anything that has the potential of being mistaken for an illegal substance such as white detergent, white vitamin tablets or powder, etc. Visually preferable substitutes can usually be found for most of these potentially troublesome items. (KAL makes a high potency liquid multiple vitamin in a brown capsule, for example.) While it can be argued that you are doing nothing wrong by carrying these perfectly legal substances, it is even more true that you do not want to do anything that draws unnecessary negative attention to you. The fact that you are innocent does little good if the official who accuses you feels forced to prove the correctness of his position by planting some of the real thing in your packet of soap.

Consider the effects of your actions on those who will be scrutinizing them. These observers include not only the range of officials and bureaucrats, but also crooks and other predators, as well as potential business associates.

Notifications and Backups

Make copies of your passport title page, visas, credit card descriptions and identification numbers, and your itinerary. Keep a copy separate from your travel documents. Leave another copy with a trusted friend or family member. Make arrangements to check in with them periodically along with instructions if you fail to make contact. Leave some flexibility in this so that the Foreign Legion is not unnecessarily called into action.

Chapter 5
The Shopping Kit
&
Other Things You'll Be Glad You Brought

Many things you need to make your trip comfortable and rewarding are available at your destination. The prices are often less than they are at home. If you know everything you need is available there, pack sparsely and bring extra cash. If you have not been to your destination before, there is no way to determine this in advance. Some things are so important that the future of your trip may be crippled if you do not have them. This chapter looks at the obvious and not so obvious bring-alongs that have proven invaluable to me over the years. At the end is a checklist that can help you organize your packing.

Luggage

Locking hard-sided luggage further sealed with a luggage strap offers the best security. Samsonite or something similar is a good choice. Avoid the heavy duty metal cases that you see couriers and drug dealers carry in the movies. This type of luggage, as well as other expensive or high security pieces, is an advertisement to the crooks that there is something interesting inside. It does not hurt to scuff or distress the outside of a new case before you use it the first time.

Try to get all of your pieces keyed the same. Most companies only have a few different types of lock and key combinations. If you compare the locks between your choices, you can find those that are keyed alike. This may not sound very secure, but the locks and the straps are only a deterrent. If a thief wants what is in your suitcase badly enough he will simply steal the whole thing. You just want to make things as difficult for him as you can.

Brightly colored luggage straps (all of the same color) make it easy to pick yours out at the luggage carousel. It is also another identifying characteristic that could lessen the chances of it being successfully stolen or aid in its recovery should it be lost.

Hard-sided suitcases give good protection for fragile pieces if they are well packed. Items wrapped in bubble wrap then put in another container inside the hard side usually have very high survival rates. I have never had any breakage of fragile Chinese trade porcelains I brought back from Jakarta packaged this way.

The greater the weight of each of your individual purchases, the smaller your pieces of luggage should be. It is hard to believe how heavy a full-sized suitcase can be when it has been stuffed with beads or silver bracelets. Test lift the luggage you are planning to bring, loaded with the types of things you are thinking of buying.

Tag your luggage inside and out. Include your name, address, phone number, and country. This gives you some hope of recovery if it is lost or stolen. If you have a mail receiving service such as Mail Boxes Etc., use that address. The best outside tags come with leather flaps over the notification information. Thieves operating from airports have been known to target overseas traveler's homes while they are gone, so it is best to keep your personal information as private as possible. The information inside can be on a business card or index card.

Duffel bags convey the possibility of greatly expanding your luggage capacity. You can carry extra ones inside each other or inside your hard-sided suitcases. The best ones are made from non-tearing cross-hatched material. The cheap ones hold up pretty well also and cost little enough to be considered disposable.

Get at least one medium-sized duffel bag made from non-tearing material to use as a buying bag. It should have an outside pocket for your shopping kit and should have both shoulder and hand straps. Whole Earth Provision is a good source for these high quality duffels.

The ideal size for your carry-on bag is just big enough to fit under an airplane seat (9"x 14"x 22"). If it is any larger than that and full, it may not fit. It should have one or more outside pockets and hand and shoulder straps. Shoulder straps are as much for security as for comfort. You can continue to hold onto the bag while it sits on the ground or wrap it around you if you grab a nap in the airport. Never turn loose of your bag.

Buy similarly keyed luggage locks for your duffel bags. Get ten or so. They are cheap.

Carefully consider what luggage you are going to bring. A carry-on bag and two hard-sided (large, small, or a combination) pieces with two or more duffels inside are usually adequate for me.

Be aware that luggage and packing materials are not available everywhere. You may not find anything suitable to carry home your treasures. Bring enough to satisfy your minimum requirements.

I was in Bolivia searching for old silver crosses and ornaments. After spending a rather unrewarding two weeks in the highland areas of La Paz and Potosi, I moved down to about 9,000 feet to the old colonial town of Sucre. I was still not having much luck with the silver when I began noticing that the local Indians were selling very interesting red and black ponchos with reversible graphic designs. I later learned that these were only made in the nearby village of Potola. The weavings were very beautiful and I bought many of them.

The small hard-sided luggage I had with me was perfect for the silver I had come to find, but was useless for these textiles. I had assumed that I would be able to find something in the market to bring then home in. I was wrong. The local people almost never traveled. There was no luggage of any kind for sale in the entire city.

I spent the better part of two days roaming the city looking for something adequate. Finally, I saw someone in a shoe store emptying shoes from an enormous duffel bag. I tried to buy it on the spot but was told to return to talk with the owner. It took quite a lot of convincing before I was able to buy it for $18. When filled with the weavings it was very bulky and weighed over eighty pounds. It was nowhere near perfect, but it carried my weavings home.

The Shopping Kit

The shopping kit has both illusionary and utilitarian functions. It will allow you to weigh, measure, and examine the things that you are considering buying. The contents also serve as symbols of your knowledge and expertise. The use of the shopping kit as a proficiency prop is discussed in great detail in Chapter 9, Making the Purchase.

The kit components suggested here are effective with furniture, wood carvings, beads, jewelry, and textiles. According to your area of interest you can add or subtract from the list.

A small calculator is one of the most versatile tools you can bring. Make certain that you either have a battery powered one (with two sets of extra batteries) or a solar-powered one with battery backup. Solar-powered calculators do not work in the dimly lit shops and alleys where you will spend much of your time. Your calculator is used to compute, communicate prices, and to make it look like you really have something to think about.

Paper and pen enable you to take notes, make sketches, draw maps, and keep records. Bring along plenty of each.

A battery-powered digital scale is essential for buying jewelry or jewelry components. Several brands are available. Tanita makes a durable assortment for about $100 on up depending on the sensitivity and range. Bring extra batteries. Most vendor's scales are accurate, but your personal scale gives you protection against the occasional crook. Most importantly it makes you look professional.

A magnifying glass affords you a better look at just about anything. One with its own built-in light with 8x power is a good choice. As you examine things with the glass you be will told about flaws that you may not have noticed.

A bright flashlight (again with backup batteries) is essential for examining larger pieces. Many flaws are hidden by the darkness. Shine the beam at different angles to help identify coverups. It can also be helpful during power outages which are commonplace in many foreign lands.

A small tape measure keeps you from having to estimate or rely on someone else's measurement when size is important.

A couple pieces of cloth can be used to handle really funky offerings or to protect a fragile treasure.

Appropriate business cards can help establish your credibility. Plain ones work as well as the fancy ones.

Keep a copy of the title page of your passport in your kit. Even in countries that require me to have my passport with me at all times, I keep it locked up and only carry a copy. If approached by an official, I hope to convince him to return to my hotel if he wants to see the actual document. There is some risk in doing this. I prefer to take it rather than the risk of having my passport lost or stolen. If you feel better having your passport with you, keep it well hidden and close to your body.

A cheap foldable waterproof poncho can save you from unexpected downpours or be used as extra packing material. I luckily had one in the mountains of Nepal that worked as a makeshift bucket to fill an overheated radiator from a stream. I don't think my driver was nearly as impressed as he should have been.

Trip Documents and Records

Organize and safeguard your trip documents and records. Letter-sized, expandable folders are useful for this. Colored, stick-on labels will help tell them apart.

The most important folder is the one containing your passport, tickets, vouchers for prepaid accommodations and services, hotel confirmations, and reserve cash. Also include currency declaration and customs information, driver's license, credit cards, keys (house, car, luggage), airport parking ticket, and a list of trip related phone numbers.

Never set down this folder. It should be in your hand, in your locked carry on bag, or in the hotel safety deposit box. Arrange for the safety deposit box as part of your check-in procedure, before you go to your room. If you are traveling with a companion have them remind you if you falter on this. That way both of you will pay attention. Keep the cash you are carrying here in several different regular envelopes. This enables you to access money without rummaging through all of it in front of the hotel clerk or anyone else who may be watching. Remove the envelopes as you need them and sort through the contents in the privacy of your room.

Set aside a folder for receipts and travel expenses. This is important if you need to document them for tax deductions. Also, check them against your credit card statements when you return to verify that nothing extra has been added.

Keep purchase receipts and summaries separately for each country you visit. This enables you to complete the paperwork required by customs or your broker.

Large manila folders usually work better than the half sizes for organizing your preliminary trip and shopping research. They can easily hold maps, book pages, market information, prospective daily plans, and a copy of your itinerary.

Odds and Ends

You may think of a lot of little odds and ends that can make your trip easier. Go ahead and bring them if it is not too much trouble.

Cheap watches are not normally targets for thieves and keep time about as well as the expensive ones. Everyone in your group should have one.

An **alarm clock** is indispensible. Set it every night. It will force you to acclimate to local time and will act as a backup when your wake up call does not happen. Do this even in the most expensive and highly regarded hotels. This is most important when you have a flight to catch. You do not want to miss one overseas. It can screw up your whole trip.

An assortment of **safety pins** can be very handy. They fasten things, remove splinters, and are useful for lots of other tasks that will not be apparent until the time comes. Remember that you have them and you will find plenty of uses for them.

Swiss army knives are as good as their reputation. Get as many gadgets as you dare. Keep them in your checked luggage. Some countries consider them weapons and confiscate them. You can get them back at your destination but it will be another time consuming procedure you endure.

Medical Supplies

Bring along an adequate supply of prescription medication and useful over the counter remedies. Prescription drugs are now available worldwide and are often significantly cheaper than here. Nonetheless, you can't always be sure that you will be able to get them when you need them.

If you wear prescription glasses take an extra pair. If it is necessary to replace them overseas it will probably be inexpensive. However, there is no way of knowing whether or not it will be possible.

Dehydration is a problem that can sneak up on you with debilitating consequences. The environment of low humidity on long airplane flights and the stress of traveling are both contributors. Consider bringing along several bottles of a sports drink such as 10K inside a Ziploc freezer bag to prevent leakage. Put one of the bottles in your carry on and drink some every hour or so of the flight. Save a bottle for your flight back. It can make a real difference.

When I first began traveling, I frequently had severe stomach cramps accompanied by vomiting which would begin shortly after I arrived at my destination. This would sometimes be very difficult to shake.

Once I had to be hospitalized in Damascus to be rehydrated by intravenous solution. This was a much more pleasant experience than you might imagine. I was brought to the hospital by the hotel doctor in his Volkswagen Beetle. He got me a bed and had the IV started before I even saw a form. The cost was more than reasonable.

When I returned to the U.S. I had extensive tests run but they revealed nothing. A friend recommended that I try drinking sports drinks with electrolyte replacements. I tried it on my next trip and it worked. I now use them religiously and have never again had a dehydration problem.

If the dry air on the plane effects your nose you can use one of the hydrating nose sprays that are available. Some travelers use a dab of Vicks VapoRub in their nostrils to alleviate this problem.

The dry air and close quarters on the plane is also a good breeding ground for colds. Antihistimines and throat lozenges can help relieve the symptoms.

I always carry antibiotics when traveling, especially when I am going into remote areas. They can be purchased over the counter in many countries. Check with your doctor for recommendations.

Secret Hiding Places

If a thief wants your money, has you isolated, has time, and has a weapon or can overpower you, he will get it. There is nothing you can do other than guard against getting into this type of situation.

There are measures you can take to protect yourself from losing all your money to pickpockets or to a thief in a confrontation. The first rule is never carry your wallet or anything else of value in your back pocket.

Actually, you should have your money spread out in several places. Some should be in your front two pockets. Small local bills should be kept in the pocket which is easiest for you to access. Larger local bills along with five hundred or so U.S. dollars can be kept in the other front pocket.

You can make these pockets even more secure if you cut the bottoms out of your regular pockets and build deeper pockets with old t-shirt material. This works particularly well with sweat pants. Not only does this help thwart pick-pockets, but it makes it less likely for you to lose something. If you are lucky enough to be able to stretch out on the plane you can twist your pocket to keep things from falling out. It does not take a lot of skill to do this sewing task, just patience.

A money pouch worn next to your body is essential. Here is where you keep your important money as well as your safety deposit key. If you insist on carrying your pass-port or airline tickets with you, this is where they should be also. You can find these pouches at travel and luggage stores.

When considering clothing for travel, look for comfort and lots of pockets. Banana Republic has an outstanding selection to choose from. The more pockets you have, the more places you have to stash things. If you have a coat or windbreaker with an inside pocket or a zippered pocket you can put your medium money there. It further removes it from the small local money you will use to buy cokes, pay taxi drivers, etc. If you wear a coat, resolve to never take it off outside your hotel room if you are using it as a cash depository.

Packing and Labeling Materials

Now that you have purchased your treasures, you want to get them home in one piece. If you are shipping them, you can usually trust your shipper to do a pretty good packing job. Let him know if any of the pieces require special attention.

The things you are bringing back yourself will need to be properly protected. A small roll of bubble wrap, Ziploc bags (preferably the freezer type that can be written on), and a roll of tape will start you on your way. Your clothing can also be used as packing material. Try to pack so that everything is secured inside your suitcase. You do not want things rolling around.

If you are bringing back a commercial-sized shipment everything will need to be labeled "Made in.....". The country name by itself is not sufficient. Contact U.S. Customs where you plan to clear to find out what currently qualifies as a commercial shipment and to verify the labeling procedure. Textile labels also require fiber content to be indicated on the label. If they are wearable you should include care instructions such as "Dry Clean Only".

Almost any printer can supply you with country of origin gummed labels in about two weeks. Sew on labels can be ordered from:

Name Maker, Inc.
P.O. Box 43821
Atlanta, GA 30378

Contact them well in advance to inquire about prices and minimums. You can also check with businesses associated with children's summer camps that provide parents with labels for clothing.

If you are using a foreign shipper he may be able to provide you with labels or he may not. It is best to have a good supply of your own.

Snacks

If you are traveling to places like Asia where the time change reverses your days and nights you may find yourself awake at the wee hours of the morning. Since this will be lunch time for your body, you will be hungry. Not all of the places you stay will have twenty-four hour room service, so a package of cheese crackers could really come in handy. You will be glad you brought a supply of snacks if you are traveling to small towns or villages or if you tire of the local food. Small, individually wrapped packages keep your snacks fresh until you need them and give you a certain amount of portion control when you are forced to share.

Books

A great book can make the interminable hours on the plane seem shorter. It can also give you something to do when you wake up too early. While books that have some connection to your destination can be motivational, it is probably better to try to select the books you think will be the most interesting. If they have a connection to where you are going, consider that an added bonus.

Look for the used book shops that seem to be springing up worldwide. Many of them have very liberal exchange policies, especially for contemporary fiction. You may be able to trade the books you read on the way over for the ones that will make your return trip bearable. Pay attention to English language books that were published in other countries. In Asia, for example, there is a lot of interesting material from Great Britain, Australia, and India.

You can carry the guide books you select in their totality or cut out the pages you feel are important to save space. Make sure to include the maps.

Clothes and Toiletries

The clothes you bring should be selected for comfort. They should also have pockets, lots of deep pockets. If you are going where it is cold, organize your clothing so that it can be layered. This is a lot more convenient and warmer than having a large bulky coat. Obviously, clothing that you can wash yourself and that dries quickly is a big plus.

Shoes should be chosen for comfort and well broken in. Your feet need to be completely covered to protect you from the unmentionable nastiness you may find yourself walking through.

Your toiletries will be divided between your toothbrush, toothpaste, and deodorant which go in your carry-on bag and everything else that will be checked through.

If you bring any small appliances you need a plug and voltage adapter. These are available at travel stores and some drug and discount stores. They range from the very simple to what appear to be small power plants. If you can get by without them, leave the electronics at home.

Checklist (Things to Consider When Packing)

(1) Luggage
   Hard-Sided Luggage
   Duffels
   Carry-On Bag
   Locks and Keys
   Luggage Straps
   Luggage Tags

(2) The Shopping Kit
   Medium-Sized Duffel
   Calculator and Batteries
   Pens
   Paper
   Digital Scale and Batteries
   Magnifying Glass
   Flashlight
   Tape Measure
   Cloth
   Business Cards
   Copy of Passport Title Page
   Foldable Waterproof Poncho

(3) Trip Documents and Records
   Small Expandable Folders (at least 3)
   Large Manila Folder
   Passport and Visas (if needed)
   Tickets
   Vouchers For Prepayments
   Hotel Confirmations
   Cash and Travelers Checks
   Currency Declaration and Customs Infor-
   mation
   Driver's License
   Credit Cards

Keys (House, Car, Luggage)
Airport Parking Ticket
Important Phone Numbers

(4) Odds and Ends
Cheap Watch
Travel Alarm Clock
Safety Pins
Swiss Army Knife

(5) Medical Supplies
Prescription Drugs
Extra Pair of Glasses
Sports Drink
Hydrating Nose Spray
Antihistimine
Throat Lozenges
Antibiotics (with your doctor's approval)

(6) Secret Hiding Places
Sweat Pants With "Deep Pockets"
Money Pouch

(7) Packing and Shipping Supplies
Bubble Wrap
Ziploc Freezer Bags
Tape
Sticker Labels (country of origin)
Sew On Labels (country of origin for textiles)

(8) Snacks

(9) Clothing and Toiletries
Comfort
Pockets
Layers
Broken In, Foot Covering Shoes

Toothbrush
Toothpaste
Deodorant
Voltage Converter and Adapter (if necessary)

———————————————

Chapter 6
Timely Information

Books, clubs and organizations, shows and exhibits, "how to" classes, and periodicals are each important sources of information. The more you know about your products, the marketplace, and current trends and events that could influence them, the easier it is for you to make good decisions.

Books

Good reference books are available for almost every area of interest. If you have no other guideline, begin with the most recent title that seems comprehensive and work back from there. Often your best suggestions for current information will come from collector organizations or user associations. Advertisements and book reviews in specialized periodicals may also point you in the right direction.

Clubs and Organizations

Clubs and organizations are sources of information and contacts. They may provide opportunities for buying or selling. You can find them by asking at businesses that sell related material and in advertisements and announcements in specialized periodicals. If there are no collector/user clubs or organizations for your specialty, consider starting one. Most of them are organized on a non-profit basis, but you could begin one informally or as a regular business. Research local rules and regulations and check with a lawyer to protect yourself from running afoul of the authorities.

Shows and Exhibitions

Attend every show and exhibition that is related to your

area of interest. This is especially important when you are starting out. You get first hand knowledge about potential competition, such as quality of merchandise, types of displays, and pricing for the cost of a ticket. Specialized periodicals are your best source of dates and locations.

"How to" Classes

Classes that teach skills such as gemstone identification, antique restoration, and picture framing offer skills that can prove to be valuable. Even if the course is only mediocre, you will seldom waste time by taking it. Contacts for buying and selling can be peripheral benefits. To find courses that are suitable for you, check with collectors' clubs, local colleges, leisure learning providers, and specialized periodicals.

Auction Houses

If you find something that you think is a real treasure, it may be difficult to find an accurate appraisal of its authenticity or value. The major auction houses will usually give you an opinion. Their catalogues are also great resources for keeping up with prices for the best pieces in your field. *Art and Auction* magazine provides names and addresses of most of the auction houses here and abroad in each issue. You can contact Christie's at 212-546-1000; Sotheby's at 212-606-7000; Butterfield at 415-861-7500.

Periodicals

Finding the right periodical for your speciality may require some effort. Many of them are little more than desktop publishing efforts. They are, however, often the bibles of their respective fields with dedicated readership. They are worth searching for. Check the nooks and crannies of the magazine rack at your bookstore. Ask at appropriate speciality shops. Look through the advertisements and classifieds of related general circulation publications.

You will find enough information about your area of speciality if you are persistent. It may be far more important to become aware of what is happening in tangentially related and seemingly unrelated areas. What's in; what's not; what's happening and where. The following periodicals present a well rounded, multifaceted view of the world:

Los Angeles Times. (Sunday edition). Pay special attention to the front section, magazines, and everything to do with entertainment or fashion.

New York Times. (Sunday edition). Front section, magazines, entertainment, and fashion.

The Economist. Financial implications of the stories that make the headlines and some that don't.

Art and Auction. The large numbers and dirty little secrets of the international art world.

Asia Week. Business has gotten big in the Pacific Rim and it is getting bigger every day. You can't afford to ignore it.

Vanity Fair. As much fashion as *Vogue* (just look at the ads) with stories about the movers and shakers, their activities, destinations, and toys.

World Press Review. Not everyone reports the same story or puts the same spin on it as our journalists. Comments from newspapers around the world.

The Village Voice. While the Voice is now some-what mainstreamed, it provides a close look at the today's New Generation. You may get better information from your local underground paper. It is usually free and available anywhere that has to do with music or alternative lifestyles.

The Wall Street Journal. Most valuable are the news summaries and offbeat stories on page 1.

This list is by no means comprehensive or exclusive. Many of these publications could easily be substituted with a similar one. Regardless of how irrelevant this material seems, you will profit by having a better understanding of what is happening in that part of the world that is outside of yours.

Chapter 7
Comfort and Safety in Faraway Places

Common sense and planning go a long way toward making your adventures comfortable and safe. Each destination has its peculiarities. It is important to consider daily preparation, health, food and drink, money, securing your property, dealing with the people you meet, communications, transportation, crisis situations, and anything else that is critical to your business or to you individually.

Daily Preparation

Review your daily plan/itinerary each night before you turn in, and again, in more detail when you wake up in the morning. Take care of any changes or special arrangements that are necessary.

Get into the habit of using both a travel alarm clock and a wake-up call to get you started each day. Take this precaution even in supposedly first rate hotels. Do not rely on your internal clock. Even when time changes are not that significant, your rhythms will be disrupted by the stress of your journey. If you take a chance you might really be surprised by how long you can sleep.

Make certain that you know what day it is. This may not be as obvious as you think if you cross the international date line. (Yes, I missed a flight because of this type of error. But only once.)

Before leaving your room, verify that everything that can be locked is locked. Check your money. Be certain you have an amount sufficient to fund the day's activities (plus a little more). Make sure that it is in the proper currencies and denominations. Keep a copy of your passport title page along with your big bills in your under-the-clothing valuables pouch. If you have reason to think that you will be required to show this copy during the the day, make another copy to keep more conveniently in your pocket.

It is also handy to have a card with the hotel name and address written in the local language to show taxi drivers for your return trip. The hotel front desk or concierge can help with this. They can do the same for your initial destination.

Health

You want to stay healthy while you are traveling. This is true for all the obvious reasons plus others that only become apparent after you become ill.

If your illness is serious, the medical facilities may not be adequate to deal with your problem. They may do you more harm than good.

Several Western travelers in Cambodia died recently after receiving contaminated intravenous rehydration solutions. Because of supply shortages, both solution bags and needles were used over and over again. This is particularly chilling to me since I have been the recipient of this type of treatment under less than ideal conditions.

Also, your medical insurance plan may not be valid for overseas treatment. Check with your insurance carrier to find out about your coverage, including medical evacuation and transportation back to civilization. This transportation can be hideously expensive and is usually not covered by regular health insurance policies. If you want this coverage you need to buy a supplemental policy. Your insurance agent can give you suggestions.

The best thing, of course, is not to get sick. Take care of

yourself. Watch what you eat and drink. Relax as much as possible. Get plenty of sleep.

Drinking alcoholic beverages on the plane can be particularly harmful. Not only does it increase jet lag, but it causes dehydration and increases your susceptibility to sore throats. (Not to mention the potential supercharged hangover.) Avoid them.

Drink lots and lots of water on the plane, even more than you want. Sports drinks can also help to replace the electrolytes you lose.

Eat sparingly. Avoid foods that are difficult for you to digest.

Exercise on the plane. Walk around every hour or so. Stand at the back of the plane and do some simple stretching exercises. This is not only to cut the boredom and make you feel more comfortable. It may help prevent serious health problems.

Doctors reported the blood clot that formed in the leg of former vice president Dan Quayle may have been the result of restricted circulation from sitting in the same position for long periods while flying.

Get off to a good start!

Remember these admonitions about eating and drinking in moderation after you arrive at your destination. You do not need to adopt a completely acetic traveling lifestyle. You do need to use good judgment.

If you get sick, do not play around. If it is a cold or something else that seems minor, you can visit a pharmacist. They have far more latitude in most foreign countries than here in the U.S. They are reasonably competent at diagnosing common ailments and in many cases can give injections if it is warranted.

If you feel it is more serious, find out if your hotel has a doctor on call or can recommend one. Most better ones can assist you. This is one reason for paying a bit more for quality accommodations. If they can't help you, contact the U.S. embassy or consulate.

Food and Drink

Sampling the local eating and drinking fare in moderation can add to the enjoyment of your traveling adventure. Making the wrong selections can be a nightmare. There is unfortunately no universal agreement on what acceptable food actually is. There can be disagreement on what parts of animals are the tastiest. Some choices could perhaps be mistaken as pets or bait by the uninitiated.

Ordering familiar items from the menu of a four star hotel that caters to Westerners does not necessarily spare you surprises. Did you know that club sandwiches can contain roast beef and a runny fried egg?

Familiarize yourself with the traditional foods of the regions you will be visiting. You can do that by seeking out the restaurants in your area that serve them or by purchasing a cookbook and preparing some choices yourself. Going to the foreign restaurant is the better choice. Sample a range of dishes. Ask for suggestions. If it seems appropriate tell them you are planning to visit their country and find out what to expect. Remember how to order the dishes you like. A phonetic spelling can be helpful.

You can usually trust dining recommendations by guide books and hotel personnel. Stay with their top picks and your overall experiences should be positive. You are not looking for fancy. You are looking for good, clean, and safe.

Resist the urge to eat off of the street no matter how tempting it appears.

If you only drink liquids from bottles that are opened in your presence without ice, you will avoid many chances for becoming ill. This includes soft drinks, water, and beer. (Avoid ice even in the best restaurants and hotels if you have any question about water quality.) Coffee and tea are probably okay if they are served very hot. Local beers are usually excellent and fairly cheap. Imports of any kind, especially alcoholic ones can be budget breaking. If you are going to order them it is wise to price them before hand. If it is possible, carry bottled water with you as you go about the day's activities. Ferreting out treasures is thirsty work.

For snacks you can look to local bakeries for safe and tasty choices. Chocolate is usually pretty good. If you want treats such as prepackaged cheese crackers, bring them with you. Avoid potato chips and the like. Even if the packaging is attractive, they can be fairly nasty.

Money

Give a great deal of thought to the handling and care of your money and other valuables. Keep most of the big denomination bills that you carry secured in a pouch or money belt. Keep small, frequently used local bills segregated from the larger bills that you may also need access to. Thieves and pickpockets are observant. The idea of being victimized is not a pleasant prospect, but do what you can to minimize the damage if it does happen.

Travelers' checks are safer than cash but lack its flexibility and acceptability. Credit cards can pay for travel related expenses such as hotel bills and airline tickets. The appropriate mix for you will depend on your requirements and objectives. Just remember. In market and bazaar land, CASH is KING.

A local guidebook can direct you to the best legal places to exchange your dollars into local currency. Usually banks and currency exchange booths give the most attractive rates. The hotel will add on a service charge that ranges from reasonable to obscene. If you are going to change a large sum, shop around for rates if there are alternatives. Do this unobtrusively. You do not want to advertise that you have a pocket full of money. Do not ask the hotel personnel or other acquaintances for recommendations!

Consider that the vendors with whom you are dealing may be delighted to receive payment in your currency. It may be preferable to delay making any large exchanges until you determine this. On the other hand, it is sometimes considered a serious criminal offense to use any currency other than the local one. This can make doing business nearly impossible if you must make the exchange at a controlled, ridiculously low rate.

Whether to try to bypass currency exchange laws or exchange money on the black market can be a difficult personal decision. In some cases it is an acknowledged way of life that is ignored. In other cases it is fine for locals, but traps are set for unwary visitors in an effort to extort money from them. If you choose to chance it, you should be aware that you could lose all of your money, go to jail, and spend thousands of dollars on fines and legal fees trying to extricate yourself from the quagmire. If you are tempted to try it, find out about both rates and consequences before you make the leap. A vendor with whom you have already done business and who you feel you can trust is your best bet for information. You then have to weigh the risks versus the possible rewards. If you are looking for the best overall general answer to the black market question, it is this: Don't do it.

You are usually required to declare the amount of currency you bring into any country. Non-compliance penalties can be severe. There can also be rules that request you to save all of your official currency exchange receipts. At the end of your stay, your original declaration and your remaining currency on hand can be compared with the currency exchange receipts. Any discrepancy may be considered evidence of black market activity.

As you arrive in the immigration area at the airport in Damascus, there are signs that inform you that all foreign currency must be declared. If you inquire about this during the processing procedure you receive no useful information. No one asks you anything about your money.

After you leave the primary immigration area, there is a currency declaration desk in the hall leading to customs. It is not always staffed. You are not requested to stop there, but this is where the currency declaration is made.

When you leave Syria, you are thoroughly searched. If you have more than a minimal amount of currency, they ask to see your declaration form. If you do not have one, they take your money. On my last visit, an oil man from Texas was relieved of $700 despite his rather vigorous protestations. His error appeared to be an honest oversight precipitated by the procedure for complying with their rules. Nonetheless, they kept his money. They allowed me to keep my $2,000, but I had my form.

Be careful if you are tempted to partially declare your funds to enable you to use the balance for black market transactions. If you are caught, the penalties can be serious.

One money trap can be avoided by keeping your hotel bill as small as possible. Hotel exchange rates are extremely stingy, usually as high as they figure they can get away with. Even if you use your credit card to settle your bill (which in most cases will assure that you get a reasonable rate) you may not be safe. Rather than let the credit card company make the currency conversion, some hotels calculate the bill in dollars using the rate they picked out of the air. Also, a service charge is often surreptitiously added to the hotel bill total whether or not you have already taken care of gratuities. Pay cash for meals, laundry, and other services whenever possible unless you are certain that it is advantageous to do otherwise.

Securing Your Property

To keep your property safe maintain a low profile, utilize safekeeping facilities, use your locks, and keep the hotel staff and others out of your room.

Do not wear your fancy jewelry, flash your money, or carry designer luggage. Any of these cries for attention are likely to be successful. If you stand out as a rich tourist, the thieves and other criminal types that are lurking about will be certain to notice you. Be low key.

Most good hotels have safety deposit boxes. If possible, ask about them when you are making reservations. Seriously think about another choice if they are not available. Get your box at the same time you are checking in. It probably doesn't hurt to mention that you want a safe place for your travel documents during the process of arranging for it. Never let anyone see you put money into the box or remove money from it. Use one or more manila or cardboard envelopes to transfer items in and out of the box. The security afforded by the new in room safes lie somewhere between locked luggage and a secure safety deposit box.

Some hotels may let you maintain a safety deposit box even when you are not there. This is not a reasonable request if you are a one time, short term visitor. It may be allowed if you are a regular guest and have a return reservation. Talk to the manager. This can come in handy when you travel away from the hotel for several days and then return. If you are traveling away from civilization, you may feel safer if you do not bring all your money and onward tickets with you. You may also be able to check pieces of luggage and packages.

The Montien Hotel in Bangkok allowed me to use their facilities as a base for more than a month at a time as I traveled back and forth from there throughout Asia. I left checked luggage with their bell staff and kept a large safety box where I stored cash reserves, valuable purchases, and airline tickets that were not currently needed. There was no charge for these services other than nominal tips and the $150 per day I spent for the dozen nights I stayed there.

Use your locks every day, everywhere. No exceptions. Make it a habit. Lock your suitcases and bags before leaving your room. If possible, stack your luggage and bags off to the side out of the way. This causes someone who wants to go through them to take a flagrant action. Hopefully, it will make your bags appear to be a more intimidating target than those scattered about in other rooms.

Keep the hotel staff out of your room. Especially housekeeping. You can make your own bed and straighten up. Catch them in the hall and get fresh towels. Then call the front desk and tell them you do not need any service. Tell the maid on your floor you do not need any service. When you leave do not turn off the television. Make sure the "Do not Disturb" sign is in place. Lean a chair in front of the door.

Most hotels in the U.S. insist that your room be checked every few days to verify that you are not conducting human sacrifices or doing anything else illegal. Foreign hotels have various policies. Do not be afraid to discuss your concerns with the management. Obviously, you do not want to talk about your suitcase full of jewels or the like, but you can tell anecdotes that have you starring as the victim. If you do not have one of your own, feel free to use mine.

Several years ago I was exhibiting at an antique bead show in Washington D.C. I stayed in a first rate hotel. (I knew it was first rate because a politician had been caught there engaging in certain recreational activities that were later deemed to have been inappropriate. I'm sure he wouldn't have selected a fleabag.) I took all of the above mentioned precautions including leaving the television on and the "Do not Disturb" sign out. That did not deter someone from coming into my room and making off with a Thai hill tribe jacket I brought back from my last Asian trip. In a rush to get back to the show I left it on my bed. Everything else was locked up.

When I found it missing, I immediately called the front desk and then security. Their primary concern seemed to be whether or not I had a receipt for the jacket with me. I wanted to call the police and have the maid confronted. They talked me out of it and assured me they would try to take care of it. I left for home the next day and contacted them by phone to no avail. At another show several months later, I learned that several other show participants had been victimized. One woman had all of her luggage taken. Apparently she raised more hell than I did. She got everything back the next day. She was the only one to recover anything.

The People You Meet

The people you meet provide some of your most enjoyable travel experiences. They are also responsible for some times of frustration and irritation. They may bring moments of sheer terror.

Guidebooks and the concierge or front desk at your hotel are good sources for information on dining and other recreational activities. Find out if any particular caution is appropriate or any specific etiquette is involved in the activities you are planning.

If you are working diligently to make your trip successful, there is not a lot of extra time and energy for having fun. Nonetheless, it is hard to resist the temptation to go out among them and sample some of the local nightlife.

Be careful! Many who find themselves in difficult situations in other countries get there by doing things and taking risks they would never consider at home. Taking the starring role in their misfortunes you will often find cabana boys, lounge lizards, ladies of the evening, and other friendly, but dangerous types. You should be more alert to potential problems in unfamiliar territory than when you are on home ground. The psychology of why some choose to do exactly the opposite would make an interesting study.

The hazards that lurk in wait for the unsuspecting are real and they are dangerous. They are also there for the aware, but at a level that is reduced in proportion to the amount of precaution that is taken.

Be conscious of what is going on around you. What are people doing and saying? Why are they doing it? Any time you begin to feel uncomfortable do whatever is necessary to physically remove yourself from the situation. Do this as politely and gracefully as you can, but do it. It is easy to excuse inappropriate behavior as a cultural misunderstanding. You may be hoping for something exotic and exciting to happen. Normal cues that would alert you to things not being quite right might be brushed aside. You are experiencing jet lag. You are vulnerable.

The Kingdom of Nepal is in the process of democratic reform. Since many of the inhabitants are illiterate, the new political parties identify themselves visually as well as by name. There is a tree party, cow party, bird party, etc. All of them advertise their corresponding symbols.

Near election dates, cars with loudspeakers blaring political slogans travel the streets of city and village alike. There are also parades. Most of them are full of smiling faces who seem happy to be out for a stroll. Others are composed of more serious participants. The leader with the bullhorn shouts the slogan; the followers chant the refrain. This group appears to be doing well. They have a symbol also. Their hammer and sickle is carved into a hillside that is visible as your plane makes its final approach to Kathmandu Airport.

I try to avoid these political gatherings. It can feel very uncomfortable to be in politically transient counties anytime near election day.

For a good look at the dark side of travel, read Thomas Thompson's Serpentine (ISBN 0-440-17611-5). This sinister tale is disturbing. It is also true. Many of the victims may have had a fair chance of avoiding their fate if they obeyed the most important rule of foreign travel safety. NEVER TALK TO STRANGERS. That is, never talk to anyone who presents himself to you invasively. If someone approaches you and starts a conversation, do not respond. How could it possibly be any of their business where you are staying, if you are traveling alone, or what you are looking to buy? Nonetheless, I have heard many travelers answer these questions and eagerly give out more information to their new found friends.

A disquieting update. According to newspaper accounts from Kathmandu and Bangkok, Charles Sobraj, the starring villain of Serpentine, is gaining his freedom from prison in India and will become a citizen there. Due to legal maneuverings, he will not be extradited to Thailand where he is still wanted for murder.

This may appear to be a paranoid and dismal view. A hard, closed manner is suitable for dealing with people who by their actions have identified themselves as predators. You may develop wonderful, long-lasting friendships with those you meet on your travels. You will encounter them during the normal course of business or other natural situations. They will not be intrusive strangers. Learn to tell the difference.

Tips for Travelers

The Department of State has compiled a series of pamphlets that deal with possible problems of Americans traveling in various parts of the world. Some of the information is covered by your guide book, but some of it is not. The pamphlets are particularly strong on social, cultural, and religious issues which can affect you. They cost $1 each and are available through the Government Printing Office at 202-783-3238 or by writing:

Superintendent of Documents
U.S. Government Printing Office
Washington, D.C. 20402

Currently, the following titles are available:

1. Tips for Travelers to Sub-Sarahan Africa
2. Tips for Travelers to the Caribbean
3. Tips for Travelers to Central and South America
4. Tips for Travelers to the People's Republic of China
5. Tips for Travelers to Cuba
6. Tips for Travelers to Eastern Europe and Yugoslavia
7. Tips for Travelers to Mexico
8. Tips for Travelers to the Middle East & North Africa
9. Tips for Travelers to South Asia
10. Tips for Travelers to Russia

Note that this last pamphlet also includes information the is relevant for travel to the former Soviet Republics of Armenia, Azerbaijan, Belarus, Georgia, Kazakhstan, Kyrgyztsan, Moldova, Tajikstan, Turkmenistan, Ukraine, and Uzbekistan. (If you are considering travel to these areas,

Intourist can provide you with information. This was formerly the only Soviet tour operator. It is still the largest but no longer directly operated by the government. You can contact them at 212-757-3884.)

Telephones, Faxes, and the Mail

The development of new technologies has positively effected the availability and quality of communication services around the world. You can now send and receive faxes and talk over a relatively clear line at the time of your choosing from just about anywhere. Your choices can be made primarily on the basis of convenience and cost.

Most major hotels offer a variety of business communication services, some on a twenty-four hour basis. Check on their availability prior to making reservations. In some countries fax and long distance services are also offered to the public by shipping and travel agents.

Make certain that you are aware of the complete cost to you before using any of the communication services. Usually the fees will seem a bit high, but if it is convenient you should probably use them any way. The reason for checking is to guard against getting totally gouged. Asking the question about the charges may save you money.

You can save money by using the most advantageous method of placing overseas long distance calls from abroad. Hotels often add unconscionable amounts, sometimes multiplying the long distance charges by several hundred per cent. Ask before you call. The cheapest method is to directly access ATT, Sprint, MCI, or other long distance carrier with whom you have an account. There is still an access fee, but you can usually save a lot on the overall cost of your call. Find out the proper procedure for doing this before you leave on your trip.

While mail service is adequate in many foreign countries, it is preferable to use a shipper or courier service for important packages or documents. Less than half of the letters and postcards I've mailed from Asia have reached their destinations.

Transportation

Getting around can be an adventure unto itself. There are many alternatives in most large towns or cities, fewer elsewhere.

The actual direct cost of your ride will rarely be of any real concern, although you should determine the cost before departing. Make sure that you and the driver agree on an amount if the cab is not metered. You may want to do this even if it is. (You can get a good price estimate for your destination from the hotel staff or more general information from your guidebook.)

It can be difficult to guard against the driver cutting himself in on a fat commission or forcefully taking you to his favorite shop. This subject is dealt with in detail in the context of the marketplace in Chapter 8, but some general pointers are appropriate here.

1. Do not discuss your plans or intentions with the driver.
2. If possible, have him drop you off at a landmark near your true destination.
3. Never allow him to take you anywhere other than where you want to go. NEVER.

The best choice of transportation is to hire a car and driver from your hotel. Normally, it is not much more expensive than using a taxi. The cars are in better shape and the air conditioner works more often than not. You may have some recourse if your driver proves to be obnoxious. Determine the hourly fees and minimums. If they fall outside your requirements or budget, try to negotiate more favorable terms.

A taxi is the next best and probably will be your most frequent choice. Agree on the charges. Use a firm hand.

Walking can be fun, informative, and efficient if your destination is convenient and the weather is good. If it is hot, cold, or raining, hire a taxi or hotel car. Unless you are sure of your situation do not walk at night. Be careful of shortcuts.

Avoid pedicabs and motorcycle engine powered tuk-tuks, etc. They do not give much protection from the elements and can be dangerous.

Buses and trains that operate in tourist areas offer fertile ground for criminal activities. If you have to use them, be as inconspicuous as you can and pay close attention to what is going on around you. Find out if there security officers on board and stay close to them, if possible.

It can be useful to rent a car and drive it yourself in areas that are spread out, such as Bali where you travel from village to village. However, you should only consider this option if you are a confident driver, have a good sense of direction, and feel comfortable using maps.

All of the safety precautions you take while driving at home should be observed plus a few more.

1. Purchase local insurance that will indemnify you if you are involved in an accident. In many jurisdictions a foreigner involved in an accident with a local citizen is automatically determined to be at fault regardless of the circumstances. If you choose to drive, do whatever you can to protect yourself from the legalized extortion that might ensue if something unfortunate happens.

2. Choose a plain common type of car. Nothing fancy that will attract attention! Make sure that it is in good operating condition.

3. If possible, try to have any markings that identify your vehicle as a rental car removed.

4. Air conditioning is not only a comfort but a necessity in many areas. It also allows you to drive with your windows closed which is an important security feature.

5. Do not leave anything, valuable or not, visible in the car. Thieves often need very little encouragement to break in. You can consider locking things in the trunk, but this is only really useful if you can do it surreptitiously.

6. Avoid driving at night.

7. AGAIN!!! Do not talk to strangers. Be very suspicious of anyone who tries to get your attention. Ploys can include asking you for help, telling you that your tire is going flat, causing a minor accident with you, offering or asking you for directions, or other similar ways of causing you to stop.

The last destination for my trip to northern Thailand was Mai Sai, a small town on the Thailand-Burma border. The distance from my location in Chiang Mai was about 200 miles and I decided to drive there in my rental car. The rules of the road in this region were different than those to which I was accustomed. Apparently the larger vehicle always has the right of way. I acclimated myself to this Darwinian practice by dutifully pulling onto the shoulder to avoid the large trucks that always seemed to be traveling at top speed.

Traffic was heavy that day because the queen mother was traveling in the area on the occasion of her birthday. Almost everyone was on or near the road in hopes of getting a glimpse of her. Every form of transportation was in use: truck, automobile, oxcart, bicycle, and motorcycle. The motorcycles often had as many as five people piled on and occasionally had caged animals tied to the back. Pigs seemed to be particularly popular. I know they were probably being driven to market, but I liked to think that their kindly owners were taking them for a ride.

The constant traffic with the variety of vehicles moving at different speeds for the entire journey was one of the most intense driving experiences of my life. I arrived safely, but practically had to pry my hands from the steering wheel.

Crisis Situations

Deciding what to do in a crisis situation is an intense personal decision that hopefully you will never have to make. Most authorities agree that you should readily give up your valuables if threatened. Do not be a hero, they say. If your life is directly jeopardized many of them suggest that you fight like hell and make all the noise you can. Determining exactly where the situation stands is the tough part.

For hostage or terrorist situations the Department of

State gives the following advice:

1. Normally, the most dangerous phases of a hijacking are at the beginning and, if there is a rescue attempt, at the end. It is extremely important that you remain calm and alert and manage your own behavior.

2. Avoid resistance, sudden or threatening movements. Do not struggle or try to escape unless you are certain of being successful.

3. Make a concerted effort to relax. Breathe deeply and prepare yourself mentally, physically, and emotionally for the possibility of a long ordeal.

4. Try to remain inconspicuous, avoid direct eye contact and the appearance of observing your captors' actions.

5. Consciously put yourself in a mode of passive cooperation. Do not complain, avoid belligerency, and comply with all orders and instructions.

6. If questioned, keep your answers short. Do not volunteer information or make unnecessary overtures.

7. Don't try to be a hero, endangering yourself and others.

8. Maintain your sense of personal dignity and gradually increase your requests for personal comforts. Make these requests in a reasonable low-key manner.

9. If you are involved in a lengthier, drawn-out situation, try to establish rapport with your captors, avoiding political discussions or other confrontational subjects.

10. Establish a daily program of mental and physical activity. Don't be afraid to ask for anything you need or want—medicine, books, pencils, paper.

11. Eat what they give you, even if it does not look or taste appetizing.

12. Think positively; avoid a sense of despair. Rely on your inner resources.

None of this is pleasant to consider. It is not what foreign travel and commerce is all about. Unfortunately, these thoughts work their way into almost everyone's mind, if only fleetingly. Confronting them head-on and objectively is the best way to deal with their specter. You are also forearmed if the unthinkable happens.

Chapter 8
In the Market

The marketplaces of the world are full of excitement and adventure. Sights. Sounds. Smells. People. Electricity. They are also full of potential dangers and pitfalls. If you are careful and alert and know what you are doing you can avoid most of the unpleasantness.

Touts and Taxi Drivers

Fortunately most of the potential hazards you will encounter involve risk to your money rather than to your person. These threats are real ones and can be difficult to avoid. Often they are invisible.

When you are in an unfamiliar market in a strange city everything often appears to be happening faster than you can keep up with. Signs are written in an incomprehensible language or are nonexistent. You are not sure which way you should go. You pull out your map or notes.

Suddenly a smiling stranger is at your side. "Hello. How are you?" he asks in English. "Welcome to ... When did you get here? How do you like my country? You are from America? Where are you going? What you are looking for?" He is very charming. He wants to help.

Take a deep breath and brace yourself. You are going to have to be rude. Or tricky. If you fail it will cost you time and money. Lots of time. Lots of money. LOTS! It may even become impossible for you to buy anything in the entire marketplace at a reasonable price.

You may not believe this. Or think that it does not apply

in your case. After all, the nice person who stopped to help you is a doctor. English student (very common). Tour guide. Policeman (if not in uniform and a badge is flashed surreptitiously, this can be very dangerous). Businessman with family in the United States. Do not believe any of it. It is not true. Not ever.

The folks who hang around markets and attach themselves to foreign visitors do it to get a commission from purchases made by these visitors. Or worse. The commissions they extract are exorbitant. 20%. 30%. 50%. More? You never really know. If one of these characters accompanies you or directs you to a shop or even if he claims to have directed you to the shop, the shopkeeper will be put upon to part with a commission that will be added to your bill. Care will be taken by both to see that you are not aware this is happening.

Why do the vendors put up with it? An accurate but not terribly revealing answer is that it is the way of the market. More accurately it is a form of extortion employed by the smiling, mannerly thugs, hooligans, and hangers-on. If the merchant does not comply, tourists are not directed to his shop. They may be told to avoid going there because the man is a cheat or that his merchandise is of poor quality. He may become unlucky in ways familiar to those who run afoul of minor racketeers everywhere. Besides, he can reason that the money is not actually coming out of his pocket. It is something to be passed on like a sales or value added tax.

The best way to deal with this is not to become entangled in the first place. Do not be responsive. Never admit to be shopping or to be interested in anything in particular. Look at your watch and say you must leave to meet friends. In Asia, speaking in Spanish while pretending not to understand English frequently has the desired effect. Under no circumstances allow anyone to guide you anywhere. Do not tell them your name or where you are staying.

Once they have attached themselves to you, with or without your consent, they can be almost impossible to get rid of. Shake your head. Say "NO!". Walk away. If someone insists on tagging along, consider stopping in a restaurant for a cold drink. If you are followed, complain to the restaurant owner that you are annoyed at being followed. If you go into a shop, stop at the front and say that you will not buy anything unless your tormentor is made to leave. Make it clear that he has nothing whatsoever to do with you or your arrival at this shop. Be calm. Be polite, if possible. Most important, be firm.

Taxi drivers are often another source of the same problem. What makes it worse is that it is impossible to avoid talking with them. If you know of a landmark or hotel near your destination, tell the driver to take you there rather than the shopping area or market. Never admit that you are going to buy anything. If you have to tell them to take you to the market tell them you are going there to take pictures. If you are returning from the market, say you have already spent all of your shopping money. Always refuse to stop at their cousin's store. Fake illness if you must. If you weaken, the best that will happen is that you will waste time and energy. You may waste a lot of it.

───────────────────────────

One of my favorite presents for myself in Asia is the gold baht bracelet that can be found at the red-roofed Chinese gold shops. This is the real thing. It looks different and feels different than the 14 karat alloy that that is foisted upon the American consumer. It is pure gold and is sold at a small premium to its gold value, similar to gold bullion coins such as the American Eagle or Canadian Maple Leaf. Asian women buy them as both a decoration and as a form of portable wealth. I like the idea.

After several weeks in Asia I arrived in Bangkok at about 7 P.M. I had an early flight back to the U.S. the next morning so I decided to stay at the Airport Hotel. After checking in, I went to the concierge and made arrangements for a car and driver. I explained I wanted to go first to Chinatown and perhaps then to Patpong. He said that most of Chinatown was now closing down early because of recent gang violence and asked why we were going there. There was no convenient way around telling him, but I took the precaution of having him stop the car before we left the hotel property. I cut him short as he began to tell me the right place to buy gold in Bangkok.

I made it as clear as I could that I had no interest in going to see his friend. I had been to Bangkok many times and I knew exactly where I wanted to go. Furthermore if he did not feel that he could conduct himself appropriately the trip would be canceled and I would discuss the situation with the hotel manager. The cost for the car and driver was about $16 per hour with a three hour minimum which I had had hoped would result in a less intrusive class of driver. He understood or at least he said that he did.

Almost as soon as we were immersed in the unbelievable Friday night traffic, he started in again. He knew much better places than the gold shops. Besides the Chinese were cheats, he said.

I had to yell at him a few more times but he gradually wound down. Sadly, the gold shops in Chinatown were closed and the traffic got worse and worse. I found exactly what I wanted at the gold shop in Patpong. Now I have the driver stop and wait for me at the Hotel Montien where I meet imaginary friends for dinner. Then I walk across the street to Patpong. It saves time and trouble.

Finding the Best Market in Any City

Many of the best shopping areas are famous in their own right, near historic sights, in the vicinity of legendary hotels, or close to local tour facilities or outfitters. Others are hidden in more unlikely locations.

Your preliminary research gives you a place to begin. Once you are at your destination check newspapers, magazines, and the telephone yellow pages to add to your prospects.

Put any of the places that are prominently reviewed or recommended at the end of your list. The premier shops and galleries have a fine selection of merchandise usually at high prices. You will occasionally be pleasantly surprised. That is why you place these at the end of your list rather than eliminate them completely.

Using these premier shops as points of departure can pay large dividends. Smaller shops spring up along the streets and alleyways near these destinations hoping to benefit from the overflow or the adventurous straggler. It is here that you want to concentrate your efforts.

Walk around noteworthy hotels, historic landmarks, old or ethnic areas of the city. Keep your eyes open. Train yourself to recognize the common characteristics of shops in which you are successful. What do they look like? What do their windows look like? How is their merchandise arranged? You can save time by avoiding places that have nothing to offer you. You can learn to identify the ones that offer the greatest potential.

Aleppo, in northern Syria, has been a trading center for millennia. I began my adventure here in the massive souks near the citadel whose presence still looms as protector of the city. This covered area which is as large as several football fields offers much to the everyday shopper of Aleppo but very little of interest to the seeker of fine unusual things. One exception is a good selection of old and new rugs, but these are difficult to export.

Next I decided to try my luck around the Baron Hotel. It was the prime place to stay when Aleppo was the end of the line for the Orient Express and was reportedly frequented by Agatha Christie, T. E. Lawrence, and other movers and shakers of the early twentieth century. I found some interesting shops near the hotel.

The old Armenian quarter, which at first glance does not seem promising, yielded a number of small first and second floor shops that were bursting with almost every type of collectible imaginable from pocket watches to weapons to old books. One fellow shopper was an antique merchant with several locations in Istanbul who was adding to his stock.

Many cities have traditional markets which have been ongoing in the same location for hundreds of years. These can be markets that are open every day like the souks of the Near East and North Africa or those that are open only one or two days a week like the Sunday Market in Mexico City or the Weekend Market in Bangkok. While there are opportunities in both types, the one or two day affairs are usually the best. They tend to have more occasional or itinerant vendors. There's nothing quite like someone who has just come in from the far frontier with a stall full of freshly found goodies.

It is usually worthwhile to travel to outlying towns or villages to look at their markets. Pay particular attention to utilitarian items that may be on their way out to make room for modern plastic, polyester, and aluminum. If you notice something that appeals to you try to figure out how you might be able to use it.

The size of some of these markets is enormous. There may be thousands of vendors. It is impossible to walk up and down every aisle or alley. Some of the markets are organized into official areas of concentration such as jewelry, rugs, copper pots, etc. Try to find a map. Lonely Planet's guide books can be particularly helpful in this regard. They are frequently the only source available.

If you are unable to find a map walk around until you begin finding things that look interesting. You do not have to examine every stall. Look for cues. Once you start to see things that grab your attention you are on the right track. Whether by design or happenstance merchandise of the same type congregates, even when the areas are not officially titled.

Walk through the entire market in grids if that is possible, while surreptitiously taking notes of items of interest. Do this at a forced march pace. Don't stop and waste time on marginal pieces while treasures lay undiscovered elsewhere.

Cover as much territory as you can. Make sure that you note the location of money changers, places to get something to eat or drink, and where the taxis wait.

After you zero in on something interesting, take your time and casually observe all of the stalls in the area. Identify the ones that look most promising. As explained in Chapter 9, you will visit these last when you are ready to actually make your purchases.

Normally, upscale mall-like shopping centers have little to offer. Many of the problems associated with highly recommended stores are present here also. Their overhead and retail tourist traffic usually leave little chance for negotiating good deals. If you work hard enough at sourcing, you will often make your purchases from the same suppliers as these shops. However, some of them will have high quality pieces that you may have trouble finding elsewhere. You will usually pay dearly for these. Even if price is not a deterrent, use your negotiating techniques to the best of your ability. Do whatever you can to distinguish yourself from the average tourist.

There are exceptions to the tourist trap nature of mall shopping. These occur when the merchant is a primary source for the item you are interested in buying. He may have a regular wholesale business in addition to the retail location you have wandered into.

The River City Shopping Center, which is connected by a walkway to the Royal Orchid Hotel in Bangkok, is a very upscale center indeed. I usually confine my activities there to eating in one of the several restaurants or browsing in the bookstore. I also take a quick walk through the antique shops on the third and fourth floors. There you can find the best concentration of antiques in Thailand with prices to match.

Several years ago I spotted some lovely silk ikat sarongs in the window of one of the shops. I stopped to look and noticed several large bales of sarongs in the back of the store. The posted price on these silks was reasonable, but not good enough for me to buy for export. I asked to talk to the owner. She was available but did not speak English. I asked her sales clerk to ask the price of 100 pieces.

The price dropped dramatically. I tried for another 20% with an offer for 300. The 100 price was best she could give she said. I said I would take 300 at that price if she would agree to sew in customs country of origin and fiber content labels. I had the proper labels with me for her to use. She quickly agreed and I was shown to the back room where there even more bales to choose from. I bought 500 pieces that time and several thousand over the next few years. Sadly the supply now has dried up. While it lasted I was able to pick through the largest supply of these fabulous antique pieces that I ever saw and pay within a few percent of the lowest prices, all in air conditioned comfort. Plus they labeled them for export. A great deal all around.

The telephone yellow pages can help you find a manufacturer or distributor that is not located in a shopping area. This might include furniture makers, lapidaries, and manufacturing jewelers among others. You can also use the yellow pages as one of your sources for contacting possible shippers. It is usually difficult to get a lot of information by phone so try to get general information regarding what they do. I ask one or two key questions at the end of the conversation to verify that we will not waste our time by getting together. I then make an appointment. You can also use yellow pages information to identify office buildings that house groups of similar businesses, particularly small jewelry designers and lapidaries.

The tensions created by the Gulf War caused me to decide to stay out of Asia until the hostilities ceased. Apparently many people decided not to travel anywhere at this time and air fare bargains began to appear. Some of them were almost too good to be true. I bought a round trip ticket from Houston to Rio de Janeiro for $556.

I was particularly interested in bark cloth from the Amazon basin and considered traveling to Belem to get closer to the source. Tourmalines and other colored stones were also on my list.

Prior to leaving I made an appointment with one of the major stone houses in Brazil. I met with the son of the founder. He was interested in setting up franchises in the U.S. and that was the relationship he wanted to discuss. The prices he mentioned were very high. That he was willing to front me half a million dollars worth of stones and finished pieces made the deal worth considering. He was polite and informative, although I was a little disconcerted that he cut his former wife out of several family photos which he proudly displayed on his desk. We parted friends but not business partners.

I visited a number of other wholesale dealers. None offered anything worth considering. Competition in Brazil is limited by a few large firms who control the colored stone business from mines to retail.

I went back to the hotel to regroup and consider my options. I looked through the phone book and was able to ferret out some independent stone cutters that looked promising.

The first stop on my new list was on the fourth floor of an office building near Copacabana beach. The elevator was broken so I had to walk up. The stone cutter had emigrated to Brazil twenty years earlier from Germany and had been trained in Idar-Oberstein. In addition to standard cuts he still did some work using old classical styles that were not currently in vogue. I was especially enamored by antique cushion cut green tourmalines. After we talked price I knew I was at the right spot. They were significantly less than what I had been seeing elsewhere. I bought quite a few pieces from him on my first visit and returned several more times during my stay. Subsequently I arranged for him to send me additional stones.

―――――――――

Finding your best sources is like solving a slowly changing three dimensional puzzle. You start by doing research and formulating a game plan. You must be willing to make changes in your strategy when things are not going as you hoped. Always try to look at the dynamics of the situation from different angles. Markets and sources that were once good become unrewarding and vice versa.

Chapter 9
Making the Purchase

You are not going to get the best possible price. No you're not, no matter how well you negotiate, no matter how well you apply the things you learn here. That is the bad news, the unfortunate truth. The good news is that you do not need the best price to be pleased with your results. You want to ensure that you do not get a very bad price. Whether or not you pay a chump price will be determined by how well you evaluate the item you are considering purchasing, how well you evaluate the vendor you are considering making a purchase from, and how that vendor evaluates you.

Before considering strategies for price negotiation, it is important to look at its very sensitive nature. With many people it is a point of honor to pay as little as possible for anything they buy. They tie up a lot of energy in the price war they create, even to the point of becoming belligerent. This is almost always counter-productive. If you concentrate only on feeling victorious, you do yourself more harm than good. It almost never makes sense to antagonize someone you are trying to do business with. Relax. Try to establish a good relationship. You will get a much better deal.

There is a rare, expensive, magical bead in the Himalayas known as a dZi. The people of this region believe that these beads, which are actually etched or decorated agates, were once alive as a strange type of insect. They believe that if one is unearthed in their field it must be quickly picked up or it may get away. Only after it has been touched does it permanently turn to stone.

If you try to talk to a shopkeeper about the price of these beads before establishing that you have an appreciation for them, you will probably be shown a contemporary bone or glass fake or may be told that none are available. After a cup or two of Tibetan tea (an adventure in itself), the conversation can be guided to the availability of these special beads. This is based on practicality rather than the dictates of some esoteric belief system. The merchants have found that tourists are not the type of customers that will spend hundreds or thousands of dollars on a single bead. Showing them these treasured pieces is usually a waste of their time.

Evaluating Purchases

If you are familiar with an item and have an idea of about how much it should cost, you can begin working on your relationship with the vendor fairly quickly. You can establish an appropriate image and begin negotiating.

It is considerably more challenging when you are completely in the dark about the value of the item you have just fallen in love with and have no idea about the way people in the market do business. The best way to navigate in these circumstances is to develop several price reference points. You also need to get a feel for the local negotiating style.

First decide what you want to use as reference pieces. Select at least two. Choose things you like that are fairly inexpensive and have some similarity to your target pieces. Do not deal with the vendor that has the best selection of what you are eventually going to try to buy. Your mission now is to <u>not</u> buy the items! This can be more difficult than it appears, especially with utilitarian pieces which may have little local value. While you will establish rapport, that you are not bargaining with the goal of buying may negatively influence the impression you make.

Your bargaining style will differ from your serious style in that you will make your offer earlier. Make your offer the first time you are prompted. This saves both your time and that of the vendor. A good rule is to decide the lowest amount you think your target piece will sell for and to discount that figure by a third to a half. Do not be afraid that your offer is too low. Make sure that it has some basis in reason but do not worry about it being reasonable. Do not move your figure and politely refuse any counter offer. After a short time pull out some money as you are getting up and restate your bid. Then start to leave. Often you will buy the object. If the vendor agrees to your price you are morally obligated to go through with the transaction. That is why you should only use things you are willing to buy as reference price items. You will end up owning many more of them than you expect. If you did not make a purchase, raise your amount by ten percent or so at your next stop. Keep careful written records of your offering price, the vendor's initial price, his last price, and the selling price if the deal was completed. Continue this process until you have both bought and failed to buy at least two different objects.

Next check your data for consistency. The percentage spread should be fairly uniform from item to item and vendor to vendor. If it isn't, you have to figure out why. For example, if the usual vendor's opening price for a particular kind of basket is $10 and you are able to buy it for $6 but not $5, you should be able to expect that you will be able to buy a $20 piece for $12, but not $10. Continue this process until you feel you have made the numbers fit and have identified any exceptions to the rule.

You now have an idea of the general price level and the spread between the asking prices and dealing prices. You can apply these spreads your target items. Since you are starting at more favorable price levels because of the groundwork you will lay, these discounts from initial price quotes should be used as guidelines rather than absolutes.

In Jakarta there is a street called Jalan Surabaya that is filled on one side with stalls of various sizes. If you come to this street early in the morning you will see a menagerie of wooden sculptures being alternately painted and wiped off resulting in a type of instant antique. There are duplicates of old United States Trade Dollars, all with the same dates and imperfections. There is also a lot of pure junk. I am sure that you get the picture. If you look like a live one, vendors will follow you up and down the street in packs hounding you to "stop for looking" in their shop. There would be no reason to come near this place if it were not for the fact that there are almost always some real gems in the rough that you just do not see anywhere else.

Several years ago while searching for 12th century Javanese beads, I stopped to look at some interesting antique ikat weavings from Sulawesi. One really caught my eye. While I liked the weaving I needed to concentrate on bead hunting. Without thinking I asked the price. "Seven hundred." I declined and went on my way.

Thus began the saga of "Wait, lady. How much you want to pay?" Things intensified when I pulled out cash at some nearby stalls and bought a few beads. I was pursued in and out of shops up and down the street for the next several hours. Finally, to rid myself of him, I told him I would never pay more than $100 for the piece he was dutifully carrying around. This was less than half of what I thought it was worth and seemed to discourage him. He dropped back into the pack. After two more hours of unrewarding bead hunting I hailed a taxi to return to my hotel. As I was getting into the cab the textile man appeared at my side and held out the lovely old piece. "How about a little more, lady. One-fifty, one-fifty."

"No,"I answered and started to shut the door.

"Okay, okay, okay. One hundred."

It is hanging on my wall today.

The point of this little tale is not that I got a very good deal on this particular textile. After shopping on this street many times I knew that you could usually expect to pay about 25% of the asking price for quality pieces. It had been a long time since I tested the market. During this period of neglectful passivity I did not notice the asking prices go from 400% to 700% of the deal price. Purchases made the next day confirmed that there indeed had been a shift. Even when you feel that you are sure that you know the local pricing structure it can pay, sometimes substantially, to verify that you are correct. Failure to do this regularly can cost you a lot of money in the long run.

Local pricing strategies can go the other way also. If one merchant begins to offer significantly lower starting prices and appears to do good business because of it, at least some of the other merchants will follow his lead.

Pricing strategies will also vary with the bargaining styles of the potential customers that come into the marketplace. Especially in tourist areas, this can change from week to week. It can make a great deal of difference whether the last group through was from the United States, Japan, or Italy.

The Right Price

Absolute prices are not as important as you might think. Relative prices are more significant, but only as they relate to your competition. Recognize that there is an upward bias on the price all the old handmade things in this world. There is limited quantity of available material and increasing demand. They will continue to become more expensive. Because of this, you need to be flexible in your price expectations. Fight the good fight, but pay the price if you really want the piece. If the price in question is high, but within reason, you make more mistakes by not making the purchase than by making it.

By the Piece or By the Lot

Often you have to decide if it is better to buy merchandise that is grouped by lot or to select piece by piece. Dealers usually prefer to sell by lot. This eliminates any guesswork for them. They can apply their markup to the whole group and ensure their profit. If they allow purchase by selection, they can be left with nothing but junk. If they have not charged a high enough premium for purchases made by selection, they may even end up with a loss.

I almost always purchase by selection even though my most profitable deals have come from lot acquisitions. If I find a subgroup of pieces in a lot that are worth the asking price of the lot, I will make the purchase. This is not a frequent occurrence. Selection is usually better.

I visited this shop in Kathmandu many times over the years. The quality was high but the prices were even higher. Several times I attempted to negotiate a purchase but the prices barely moved. The young manager told me to return when his older brother was there. He was the boss and could possibly give me a better deal.

After looking at the shelves of impressive Tibetan antiques, I asked the younger brother if he had any old beads other than the sparse selection in the cases. He pulled out a large sack from behind the counter to show me. He told me they were getting out of the bead business.I began to sort through the beads and was about halfway through when the elder brother appeared. After speaking to his younger brother, he told me that he since he was no longer going to sell beads I could only buy these as a complete lot. He quoted me a price he said was final. I could take it or leave it. The price was great. It came to little more than the value of the beads I already selected, with many obviously good pieces still remaining.

I paid him and asked if there were any other beads he wanted to show me. We went through three more bags of ancient stone beads, all of which were priced at steep discounts to their value had they been sold a few at a time. This was a great deal for both of us. I bought a large collection of beads at a fraction of their market value, while he liquidated inventory he no longer wanted.

These suggestions apply to unusual, one-of-a-kind pieces. Buy your selections as a group if you are trying to buy a large number of similar or inexpensive items. There is less opportunity for you to be squeezed for marginal amounts on each individual purchase. These can add up. If you buy by group, it is more difficult for the vendor to wear you down. You are usually operating under time constraints while he is not.

Expensive Stories

Everyone wants to know as much as possible about the magnificent treasure they just acquired. Soliciting stories or even listening to them before the deal is done is one of the most expensive mistakes you can make. This gives the dishonest dealer the perfect stage to strut his stuff and can tempt the honest man into telling you what you want to hear.

It is your fault. Not that the seller lied to you, but that you gave him the opportunity to do it. Make your purchases based on what you know or what you like. If you do not trust your taste or judgment, add to your knowledge and experience. If you rely on what a seller tells you to make your buying decisions, it will cost you money.

Written certificates of authenticity are worth next to nothing. In fact, preprinted forms may be an indication that something is amiss. Remember the trade in fraudulent fine art prints that was exposed several years ago. Prices were in the thousands for each print. When the misrepresentation was discovered, the certificate holders were left with no one solvent to stake their claims against.

Dealers, merchants, etc. can be sources of your best and most interesting information. This is not a contradiction. It is all in the timing. You are most at risk when you ask for information before the sale is complete. Afterwards you can ask as many questions as you want about what you bought. If the sale is not contingent on some particular information about the piece, you are much more likely to get a true story.

If it sounds like I am recommending that you buy things before you ask anything about them, this is absolutely true. If a dealer begins to tell me a tale about a piece I am examining, I will stop him by saying that I am only interested in it for its decorative beauty. Whether or not it was once the gift of the princess to her forbidden lover the day before he was beheaded has no bearing on its value to me. Close the deal and then let him tell his tale. This will save you lots and lots of money.

If you develop your eye and use appropriate pricing guidelines and negotiating techniques, you can buy the things you like at good prices even if you are not completely sure what they are. Buying a piece that you are intrigued with is a lot smarter than buying a story you are intrigued with.

Multiple Purchases

After you buy something from a vendor AND feel good about the purchase, you can relax a little bit. Ask him what other things he has that might interest you. You may now see something special. If you do not like anything he shows you, tell right away. There is no reason to waste your time or his. If you see any possibilities, ask about a piece you do not care about first and quickly pass on it. Then go to your target piece. The starting price should be reasonable. If it is, make the purchase.

Your buying conditions are now favorable and you

should press your advantage. If there are other things you want, try to buy them as a group. If the money involved is substantial, bargain vigorously. You have already established yourself as an important customer who is ready to spend serious money. The seller should give you a good deal at this time. If not, move on.

Cash

Cash is not a four letter word. If you want to make your best deal, get used to using it. Sellers love it. When you use cash you remove additional risk and expense from his end of the transaction. Checks can bounce. Credit cards can cost him up to 5% or more. Cash makes doing business with you much more pleasurable. Let him know it is your preferred method of payment. This is especially true in small to medium sized purchases.

You also must determine what kind of cash to use. Compare the exchange rate available at banks and money changers with what the shopkeepers will give you.

Before you use U.S. dollars or any other external currency in the market make sure that you know what money exchange regulations are in effect. Be aware of both the official rules and the practical day to day manner in which they are enforced. It is possible to save money in grey area situations where the officials turn their heads to minor exchange infractions, but you can lose all your money, go to jail, and spend thousands of dollars on legal fees and fines if they take things seriously. Sometimes currency exchange traps are set to extort money from unsuspecting foreigners by real or fake police. If you find yourself caught in one you may have little choice but to pay up. The safest advice is always use correct official channels to exchange money unless you have compelling reasons to do otherwise.

Regardless of what currency you use, you need an

assortment of denominations segregated in different locations. Specific recommendations for concealment and general safety precautions are given in Chapter 7.

If it looks like the decision is going to be a close one for the seller you can try to close the deal by holding the correct amount of cash out as you make your final offer. It also gives you something to refer to as you say "This is all I am going to pay." It should be obvious why this is more effective than making the same offer while asking to get change back.

The Bargaining Dance

There are as many bargaining techniques as there are buyers and sellers. The best of them have a sense of rhythm through which the master can lead his partner from step to step gracefully and effortlessly. There are times when you want to facilitate a smooth and even flow and other times when you want to stop the music.

The first few minutes you spend with a vendor are often the most important. During this time he will consciously or unconsciously categorize you. Once you have been pigeonholed it may be difficult for you to improve your position.

A typical dealer's hierarchy might go something like this: family members; very close friends and important long time customers; prospective important customers; prospective small customers; fools with money that needs parting; lookers. Your goal is to be treated as if you are in the second group (very close friends and important long time customers) or at least the third group (prospective important customers).

How you do things and which things you choose to do determine your status. Both of these are important, so you need to train yourself to be conscious of your progress in each simultaneously.

First we will examine the How. All natural-born sales-men have an ability to establish instant rapport with perfect strangers. In many cases they are capable of making new acquaintances feel they have been friends for a long time. For most of those capable of instant rapport, this is the way they have always dealt with situations. They do not think about it. It is natural for them. Fortunately this is also something that can be studied and learned.

Neuro-Linguistics Programming or NLP attempts to determine the essential parts of successful performance and then construct models which can be followed by those wishing to duplicate that success. Several NLP authors have written books that suggest various techniques for improving sales and other business communication skills. Influencing With Integrity by Genie Z. Laborde is the best I have seen. It is comprehensive and is also an enjoyable read.

NLP experts point out that most of us are comfortable with those we perceive to be somewhat like ourselves. Creating this feeling of similarity can be accomplished by subtlety duplicating your counterpart's postures, breathing and movement rhythms, or vocal tone. This is something that requires a certain amount of discretion. You do not want to alienate someone by making them think you are imitating them or making fun of them. Fortunately, unless you overly accentuate the mannerisms, you will establish common ground at an early stage of negotiation.

This requires some practice before you are comfortable doing it. Begin by watching how others adapt their manner-isms to fit those of the people around them. If you observe yourself you will find that you do the same thing uncon-sciously. This should make you feel less artificial when you take these actions purposefully. You will have more control and awareness of how your actions affect the behavior and perceptions of others. These techniques can be used manip-ulatively. Your new perception will help keep you from being a victim.

Body Language

When you are not conscious of yourself as you interact with others it is possible for almost anyone to determine your state of mind. This becomes obvious from your posture, facial expressions, vocal tone, and body movements. A careful observer might get additional information from your eyes, breathing and level of concentration. If they have the ability to evaluate their observations, this may give them a great deal more information than the actual words you are saying. This has both positive and negative implications. If your primary goal is to transmit information, expressiveness is very desirable. If you are in the middle of an important negotiation it can be disastrous.

If you do not engage in face to face negotiations on a daily basis, learning to hide your feelings is more important than trying to gauge the intentions of your counterpart. Concealing intent is also more important for the buyer than the seller. By having the item in his shop the seller demonstrates his willingness to sell it.

The best technique you can use for disguising your intentions is to standardize the way you examine items and request price information. Think about what you have done in the past. If you have not considered this before, it is almost certain you have given away valuable information to the merchants you buy from. This has undoubtedly cost you money.

The best way to set the appropriate tone for your future standard is to imagine that a friend has shown you a piece and has asked for your opinion of it. At first glance it looks okay, but it is not something you would buy for yourself. You know that it fits your friend's taste so you take a minute to look at it. Concentrate. Really imagine that you are doing this. Visualize the friend and the actual piece. How do you feel while you are doing this? What is your expression? Exactly how are you touching it? What do you say? How do you say it? How do you react to the price when it is given?

This is the effect you want to achieve. You are trying to convey an impression of polite indifference. You have examined the piece and it has aroused no buying passion in you. The degree to which you are able to successfully accomplish this will strongly influence your shopping success.

Never look at your most coveted item in a shop first. Always mix in some items of little interest. If you are performing correctly, the shopkeeper will not know what pieces you really want.

Practice the visualization process until you can call up the indifferent feelings and movements. This will save you lots of money.

Paying attention to body language is always useful. There are observable differences from person to person. You can pick up patterns if you look for them. Is there a certain mannerism that is evident when they reach their lowest price? Is there a particular way they handle a defective piece of merchandise?

Sometimes it may be easier to assess the true status of a bargaining situation when you do not share a common language with your counterpart. Try to determine which portions of the seller's actions are social, which are informative, and which are manipulative. If you watch closely, you can determine their intent without having to deal with words which may only mislead you.

I Say, Then You Say

Regardless of where you are in the world, there is an

expected pattern of negotiation that goes something like this. You pick up an item and ask the price. The seller quotes you a figure. You make a counter offer. He asks for a little more and you agree. Both of you smile, money changes hands, you walk away with your trinket. You never want to fall into this trap. If you do your results will range from poor to disastrous.

You must take control. One fairly easy way to do this is by breaking the rhythm. This can be accomplished by failing to respond in the way you are expected. After the vendor gives you a price, do not make an offer of your own. You can talk about the characteristics of the item or ask about other items but do not say anything about the price.

This may seem trivial but it is very powerful. That you are not responding in a familiar manner begins to loom larger and larger. It almost seems to take physical form. Your negotiating partner will feel anxious and confused. If you do a good job of establishing rapport with him, this anxiousness and confusion is not directed at you but manifests itself internally. He wonders what he did wrong. He is concerned he did not communicate clearly with his new friend. He may try to help you do your part. "I say, then you say," you are eventually advised.

However this goes, your initial offer has a much greater impact the longer you wait before making it. By being unresponsive, you subtlety take the play away from him. He will feel that it is more difficult to persuade you to raise your offer since it took so long for you to make it. He is not on familiar ground. The great thing about this tactic is that you execute it without doing anything aggressive.

Just a Little More

Whenever you hear the words "Just a little more", you can be positive that the the most recently mentioned figure is acceptable. This phrase is usually uttered in a whimpering voice and with the look of a dog hiding in the corner with his tail between his legs. You do not have to pay another penny. The deal will be done. This does not signify that you have made a great deal. It only means that it is okay to stop. Your bargaining partner may just feel that you will not go much further and that this is the best way to squeeze out that last little bit. He may have been willing to agree to the deal 30% back if you had done your job better.

Using Your Tools

Properly using the tools in the shopping kit described in Chapter 6 is the other important part of correctly positioning yourself. The premise is simple. You wish to appear to know what you are looking at and to be capable of assessing its quality. Whether this is true or not is secondary. As long as you do not do something as obviously stupid as trying to measure a diamond with a yardstick, any technologically aided scrutiny you give makes a favorable impression. The more comfortable you are with your inspection tools the better. It also helps if they are unique technological masterpieces that are not available locally. If they are desirable enough and are applicable to the inspection task at hand, the vendor may become obsessed with getting some for himself. This will have the effect of not only favorably turning the tables on your relationship, but will almost certainly give you the expert status you desire.

One measuring device that has proven useful as a give away item in the hinterlands is a pocket postal scale. They cost a dollar or so and are appreciated by traders going into very remote areas who do not have access to digital scales and for whom balance scales are not convenient. While they are not a big deal, making this type of gift helps create a positive atmosphere.

The most important use of your tools will be as props. Of course you will consider whatever information you discover during your examination. On occasion this will keep you from buying damaged goods or may help you identify a hidden masterpiece. However, the major benefit will come from the impression your examination makes and the responses it elicits.

Carefully inspecting an item or two while failing to respond to the pressures designed to get you involved in the bidding can pay great dividends. If there are some items of questionable authenticity, this may be pointed out to you lest it be discovered by your careful perusal. Similar pieces of better quality may be pointed out. Treasures under the counter or in the back room may be revealed.

The Calculator Speaks

Your calculator can be a very effective communication device. In some transactions it can make language superfluous. You can pass it back and forth as offers and counteroffers are made. You may gain at least a symbolic advantage if the calculator is yours. It might even help if the keyboard is not standard and is a bit difficult to operate. Do not just punch the amount of your offer. It should be obvious that you are actually calculating something, even if you are only adding two numbers together to arrive at your current bid. The calculator says it is worth this much and no more. It is like having an objective third party on your side.

Your offer should never be an even figure. Round numbers appear to come off the top of your head while a carefully pondered and calculated odd amount gives the impression of being more serious. The more credible the amount you offer appears to be in your eyes the greater difficulty he will expect to have in raising it.

Practical Give and Take

You probably have several impressions about the bargaining process at this point; that it is going to be like participating in a continuous war, that it is going to be difficult, and that it is not very much fun. You may also worry that everyone you meet is dishonest or conversely, that you will be doing things that are designed to take advantage of those you are dealing with. Very little of this is true.

Consider all of these strategies, but only use the comfortable ones. Even these can be added gradually, in stages. The confidence you get from knowing that you have some control over what happens makes your shopping experience more pleasant.

The degree to which you feel you are involved in a war depends on the strategies employed by you and your counterpart. Being aware of the conflicts involved provides you with the ability to protect yourself. Your control of the situation keeps you from experiencing that gnawing sensation of being manipulated. You are not compelled to act defensively. Bargaining takes place in an atmosphere of mutual respect.

Most of the people in the marketplace are similar to those you deal with anywhere. They are basically honest with varying degrees of inclination to take advantage of you should the opportunity arise. The more formidable the persona you project, the less likely you will be targeted as a potential victim. You can look at some of these tactics as defensive shields.

You do not need to be concerned about taking advantage

of the vendor. The cost of any item and the minimum selling price are always known quantities. No item will be sold for a loss because of your exploitative bargaining tactics. This is true no matter how impoverished the vendor appears. Sometimes the illusion of poverty is adopted and called to attention because the seller has learned that this ploy is worth another 20% in profits. The vendor does not require your protection.

This somewhat hard line is applicable in situations involving serious money. What constitutes serious money to you is something that you will have to determine. For smaller purchases do not waste your time. Perhaps make one slightly lower counteroffer. If the original figure seems reasonable, consider just paying it. However, you should be forewarned that such magnanimous behavior may be rewarded with future price creep. In fact, there are some places where accepting an early offer too quickly can result in that offer being withdrawn.

I was in Jakarta at the end of an extensive Southeast Asian buying trip. My important buying was finished along with the packing and shipping. I was tired and ready to go home the next day.

While wandering around the streets near my hotel I spotted some stone and silver rings in a small shop. There were about thirty of them. The silver work was rather plain and not all that great, but the stones were spectacular—agates, rutilated quartz, other unidentifiable exotic specimens. I asked the price. His reply of about $12 each was a good one but not ridiculously low. I told him that I would take all of them and started to reach for my money.

He hesitated and began to smile. "Do you also want to buy the settings?" he asked.

"What do you mean?"I responded.

"Do you want to buy all the rings? The price I gave you was only for the stones.

I was obviously being had. I tried to treat it as a joke, but he was serious. I spent at least ten minutes arguing with him about the absurdity of quoting a price on part of a finished ring.

I found myself getting angrier and angrier, with myself for letting this happen and him for being a jerk. He was having a grand time.

Finally I started to walk away, expecting him to stop me and complete the deal. His only consolation was to tell me I could have them for only $3 more. I felt like telling him what he could do with his rings.

I walked around the area for another thirty minutes then stopped back by his shop. He found the situation funnier and funnier. The price remained at $3 over his initial quote.

I did not buy the rings. There had been no misunderstanding. After I had jumped at the first price, he felt it was a good gamble to try to hold me up for more.

If you explore the markets in enough places you will find a few vendors who never bargain in good faith. Usually this happens in remote areas where there are only a few dealers with material of interest. Their philosophy is to quote a ridiculously high price and wait until a rich, unaware tourist comes along that is willing to pay it. These hinterland prices may be five hundred percent more than a comparable item costs in a large city in the same country.

You can avoid this by concentrating your efforts in areas where there is some competition. While there are treasures to be found in outlying villages, most of the best items find their way to a commercial centers where they have the best chance to be sold.

Long Term Relationships

After you settle into a regular buying routine, you can begin to ask compatible dealers to save things for you. You may want them to actively search for particular items. You benefit by saving time and choosing from a superior selection. The downside is that the asking price may creep up on your set aside choices or you may be expected to buy pieces that you do not want.

Communicate the exact specifications and offering prices for your selections. Start small. You can offer a small premium if it enables you to build a beneficial relationship. Carefully monitor the results of the relationship. If there are problems in price or quality, discuss them freely. Some of these associations last a long time. Others never seem to get off the ground or quickly fade.

The area they call the Witch's Market on Calle Sarganaga in La Paz is really not all that interesting. Besides, the old Aymara Indian women tending the stalls do not like uninitiated Westerners poking around in their wares. I doubt if any of us have purchased the dried llama fetuses or herbs they sell for use in their folk medicines.

Down the hill toward Avenida Mariscal de Santa Cruz the street is lined with vendors selling jewelry, antique coins, junk, and weavings. This is where I met Hortencia back in the mid 1980s. At that time old collectible weavings were mixed in with new ones and sold for about the same price. Hortencia had the largest and best selection of old pieces. She was also easy and pleasant to deal with. I spent a lot of time and money with her.

At the end of one of my trips I suggested that I would write to her in advance of my next trip to let her know if I had any special requests. She thought this was a good idea. Several months later I sent her a letter with photos of my favorite styles.

She was the first vendor I visited on my next trip. She proudly showed me the sack of shawls and ponchos she saved for me. They were beautiful. We counted them together and I got out my money to pay her. She started shaking her head. These special pieces were "otro precio" which she calculated to be about 30% over the regular rate. There was nothing remarkable about these pieces except than I liked the patterns. They were not older or more special than any of other pieces she had for sale. In her mind my request had made them more special and therefore, more expensive. After a few minutes of unsuccessful negotiation I left her stall to try my luck elsewhere.

I made several purchases at normal prices at

neighboring stalls. After watching this for awhile, she called me over and sold me the weavings at the regular price. I made some additional purchases from her, but our relationship was never the same.

━━━━━━━━━━━━━━━━━━━━━━━

Her actions seemed perfectly normal to her; to me they seemed like opportunistic price gouging designed to take advantage of me, her best customer. Of course, this situation was completely my fault. I had not considered how my actions would affect her. This was a valuable lesson for me.

My recent efforts have had better results.

━━━━━━━━━━━━━━━━━━━━━━━

I met Lobsang and Tenzin several years ago on the final day of my in stay in Pokhara. Pokhara is located on a lake in the foothills of Mt. Annapurna and is the site of the summer palace of the king of Nepal. It is also a stopping place for Tibetan pilgrims on their way to Dharamsala to see the Dalai Lama.

On our first meeting I bought several beads from them and arranged to contact them through their cousin who works in a local hotel. At first I looked at what they brought me and bought what I wanted. Each of them owned some of the pieces individually; together they owned others; sometimes they brought consignments from family and friends.

Gradually, I began making requests for particular items. I started with inexpensive prayer malas and worked up from there. The few times they tried to press up their prices past market levels, I expressed my displeasure and sent them on their way. Over the years we developed a good working relationship and they became one of my best suppliers.

A Final Word on Buying

Whenever you get a funny, uncomfortable feeling about a piece you are considering or the person who is selling it, STOP IMMEDIATELY. Leave. Say you are not feeling well or whatever else seems appropriate. But make certain you leave without completing the transaction. You can always come back later. Even if you occasionally miss out on buying something, you will come out far ahead if you stop whenever things do not seem right.

Chapter 10
Getting It Safely Home

Moving your treasured purchases safely from one country to another is the scariest part of international trading. This is especially true if large amounts of money are involved. You can make your best efforts to smooth the way, but there are times and places where all of the tension that you feel is justified. There is unfortunately no way around it.

Uncertainty that is both inherent and contrived is present every step of the way in the shipping and customs process. It is especially infuriating that there is usually a process that would allow everything to flow smoothly, safely and simply. The trouble is that no one seems to know exactly how all the pieces should go together. Either that or the ones that know are not motivated to tell.

The key to wending your way through this mine field of bureaucracy is preparation. The time to prepare is not the morning your return plane is scheduled to leave. This is true whether you have a bag of costume jewelry in your suitcase or four container loads of antique furniture to ship.

U.S. Customs Preparations

There are few problems with the details of entering your shipment once it reaches the U.S. if you make proper preparations. These include arrangements with a customs broker, verification that all documentation is in order, and confirmation that nothing in your shipment is prohibited.

Many first time importers and some with experience try to avoid dealing with brokers and paying duty on their imports. This is done by underdeclaring their shipments.

This is not a good idea. Hiring a broker is not terribly expensive. Duties are waived for many of the types of things you buy. Most duties are not exorbitant in any case. If you are caught doing something stupid like this the penalties can be severe.

It may appear that brokers do little for their money, but they are a valuable source of information and they can smooth the way if they are good at their job. Besides, it is the way things are done. If you spend a lot of time worrying about how things ought to be in this part of the business you will get an ulcer at the very least.

If you bring in less than $1,400 worth of merchandise with you or ship less than $1,000 you probably do not need a broker. This will undoubtedly change from time to time. To be on the safe side check with U.S. Customs or a broker before you go.

Selecting a broker is like selecting any professional. Try to schedule an appointment to meet with prospects. Most are happy discuss their services. If you reach one that is too busy, call another one. There are lots of them around.

When you meet with your prospective broker, tell him where you are going, what you are considering buying, and whether you are planning to ship or carry your purchases back with you. Discuss his fees, the Customs bond, and documentation requirements. If you carry your merchandise back with you find out if he can have someone meet your plane. There is an extra fee for this but it enables you to clear your treasures immediately. Otherwise they will be held in bond in the customs warehouse for a day or two until they can be cleared. I have done it both ways without any mishaps, but it always feels better to have everything cleared and in hand.

This is a happy story from the gray area of shipping and customs. My broker in Miami had been in the business for most of his life. After working for a large shipping company in the New York area he semi-retired to the sunshine state to enjoy his golden years.

He met my flight to clear the commercial part of my luggage. It was not possible to fax him any information so he did not know what to expect. I had gone to South America to search for silver crosses and ornaments, but returned with duffel bags full of weavings.

I knew there were no quota restrictions from any of the countries I visited so I was not worried about that. I also knew that the textiles would probably have to be inspected by the customs expert. Since the experts are almost never located in the airport I knew that it was very unlikely that my shipment would be able to accompany me as luggage.

This would result in air freight charges of several hundred dollars and take some time. The prospects did not appear promising.

My old broker was a wily rascal. He made it his business to know everybody. He knew about their families and always inquired about them. I never saw him arrive in the customs area without a box of donuts or cookies which he passed around. He pleaded, wheedled, and cajoled. When necessary he would call downtown on his cellular phone.

The examining agent we drew was a large, humorless woman who immediately called attention to the necessity of having expert approval. As he pleaded our case other agents began making jokes about the situation. It was obvious that we would have no luck. Suddenly she seemed to find fault with one of the entry classifications. They argued back and forth. It looked serious.

Finally he agreed to her demands to change them. It cost another $28 in duty. I suddenly realized that the weavings were cleared. Later he told me that he was almost always successful in dealing with this woman if he picked an argument with her that she could win. He intentionally misclassified the weavings.

Most customs agents do not go out of their way to make your life miserable. Unfortunately this is not always true. For example, Seattle and Dallas have both proven troublesome for me in the past. If you have a tough time at one port of entry, consider trying another one on your next trip. There can be a great variation in the attitudes of the agents from city to city.

Prepare for customs clearance by providing your broker with copies of documentation before you arrive. This is imperative if you want him to meet you to clear customs with your carry-along purchases.

The easiest way to transmit this information to him is by fax. There are very few places in the world today where that is not possible. If your hotel does not have fax capabilities try at others. Most cities and even towns and villages have business service centers which provide fax, copy and secretarial services.

Your fax should include detailed flight information, copies of all invoices, GSP documentation, and a summary of the merchandise broken down by country and general category. If you are not sure exactly how to divide everything into categories, try to do what seems logical and give good descriptions. Consult with your broker before you depart to ensure that you know what he needs.

Receipts are important. You need them to document your purchases. Get one for every purchase if you can. This is not always possible when shopping in foreign markets. If you are unable to obtain receipts, keep a detailed written record of your purchases. When you are done buying you will make out your own pro forma invoice. I usually divide mine by market or city. I combine this with the receipts I have gotten to complete the country summary. The pro forma invoice should be as detailed as possible. If the receipts are not in U.S. dollars, make a note of the exchange rate of each country in your cover letter. All of your summaries should be in U.S. dollars.

After you send your fax, call your broker to verify that he has received it and to find out if he needs any more information. Do everything you can to take the uncertainty out of the customs process.

GSP Documentation

The General System of Preferences (GSP) program allows certain products from underdeveloped countries to be imported into the U.S. duty free. Arts, crafts, and other handmade items from many countries may be included. Check with Customs or your broker for current information.

To be considered for duty free entry under this program, your purchases have to meet GSP specifications and be accompanied by GSP Form A which is a certificate of origin. This will be easy if you are dealing with a merchant that frequently exports to the U.S. Most shippers can also handle GSP documentation even if you are combining purchases from several sources. Remember to request it.

The situation can get a bit more complicated if you buy a few pieces each from a variety of vendors and plan to secure the documentation yourself. You have to find the appropriate government official, bring him a description of the items or perhaps the items themselves, and hope that he finds no fault with your purchase of them.

Genuine antiques can enter the U.S. duty free without GSP Form A as long as they do not violate any restrictions. While they can be included in GSP documentation prepared by a merchant or shipper, avoid presenting them directly to foreign officials. It is too easy for them to raise a grey area warning.

The end was near after almost a month of travel in the Bolivian altiplano. I had been to Potosi, Sucre, and Cochabamba and was now back in La Paz on Monday afternoon. My return flight to the U.S. was scheduled to depart Wednesday morning.

I began work on solving the packing puzzle and organizing my receipts. I had never acclimated to the altitude and the lack of oxygen at over 11,000 feet made my thinking a bit fuzzy. Progress was slow as I switched back and forth between tasks.

This was before I learned the value of focusing

my buying. My eclectic collection included new silver earrings, old silver buckles, old weavings, and new handbags made from fragments of old weavings. I finally totaled everything by category. (Silver earrings, silver buckles, handcrafted shawls, handcrafted purses)

Before leaving La Paz for my journey around the country, I obtained the address and telephone number for the government office that was responsible for issuing GSP Form A. It was connected to their equivalent of the Department of Commerce. I called and tried to make an appointment for the following morning. They told me to come to the office after 9 AM.

The office was just a few blocks from the Plaza Hotel where I was staying. I walked over and arrived a few minutes early. The receptionist did not understand what I wanted. I'm not sure if this was because nobody had made such a request before or because my Spanish was poor. Finally she understood and led me to an office several doors down the hall.

I was greeted by a pleasant man who immediately understood what I wanted and got a copy of the form from his desk. He told me he could take care of everything but wondered why I was not using a shipper. I gave him copies of the invoice summaries I constructed and explained that I planned to carry everything back in my luggage. He told me to return at noon. The form would be ready then.

I returned to his office at the appointed time and was escorted back to the same office. He smiled, asked me to sit down, and held the form out for me to see. It looked fine just fine.

He explained that he was supposed to visually inspect the items described in Form A and gave me a summary of all the work he had done to prepare my document. I would save a lot of money since I would not have to pay duty back in the United States, he said. He pointed out that we were now ten minutes into his lunchtime as he held the document provocatively in front of me.

I proffered the Bolivian equivalent of ten dollars as compensation for his extra effort and we exchanged pieces of paper. The GSP Form A performed as advertised and I paid no duty.

When I later recounted this tale to a Bolivian shipper, he told me I was lucky. The old textiles and perhaps the old silver were inhabitants of the dreaded grey area and may have been confiscated. He told me that it was much safer for me to ship my purchases back to the United States through him.

When I asked why it was safer to ship through him, he said that he always had all export documentation approved for sensitive cargo before he put the package together for shipping. If Customs requested an inspection, he voided the shipment and waited a few days before he tried to get it through again.

Clearing U.S. Customs

On the customs form you receive on the plane, first list your personal purchases. On a separate line write "commercial shipment" and its value. Keep your personal receipts with a written summary in one folder and your commercial documentation in another. It may seem like too much trouble to do the summary and organization of your personal receipts but it shows that you are taking the customs process seriously. It starts the procedure positively.

Your broker will meet you in the baggage examination area after you have cleared immigration and retrieved your luggage. If you do not see him right away tell the examining agent that a broker is meeting you and find out where they wait. Always have your broker's phone number and plenty of change with you. You will not be allowed to use customs' telephones. If your broker is not there customs will usually allow you to wait for him. Sometimes they threaten to make you leave your shipment in bond, but if you are pleasant and plead with them they will give you some time.

When it is time to have your baggage examined, keep your documentation ready in hand. Present it to the agent along with your passport and customs declaration. If you use a broker he will enter the information into the U.S. Customs computer.

The agent may then ask to see various items. He will occasionally want to completely go through your things. He may ask you to move everything to a small room adjacent to the main examination area. This does not mean anything is wrong. It actually protects you from other passengers looking at your possessions. Respond politely and truthfully to the examiners questions. Do not volunteer anything. This is not a social occasion and you want to be done with it as soon as possible. After you have cleared commercially at the same port of entry several times, Customs will probably only look through your shipment periodically.

If there is any duty on your personal items you are directed to the Customs cashier. The duty must be paid in U.S. dollars. They now accept credit cards.

The duty on your commercial shipment is guaranteed by your Customs bond and will be paid by your broker. This duty payment will be added to the amount he bills you later.

At the time you establish your relationship with the broker make application for a customs bond. This bond guarantees the government that they will be paid any duties that are owed. The cost to you will depend on the amount of the bond and whether you selected to have a continuous bond or one that is valid only for one entry. The minimum amount is normally sufficient. It is usually cheaper to be bonded for each individual entry unless you are traveling more than three or four times a year or have commercial shipments sent to you that frequently.

Several weeks after entry you will receive a bill from the broker for his services and for any customs duties and fees. Accompanying this will be a copy of all the documentation and the brokers worksheet specifying the classifications. Make a note of the classifications. If the duty was minimal you want to ensure that if you import the same items again they will be entered the same way. If the duty seems large, you may want to determine if there is another classification that could have been used. Verify that all duty free GSP items have been correctly classified. Reclassification may be possible if the item involved was one that was difficult to classify or if it was a bona fide antique that was misclassified as contemporary.

The same broker has processed my West Coast customs clearances for more than five years. Most of my shipments contain handcrafted items from developing nations which are duty free under the GSP program. My brokers' invoice is normally less than $300 which includes regular brokerage services, overtime, and customs' bond.

You can imagine my surprise at receiving my latest bill for more than $4,000. The broker who processed my shipment did not enter my shipment as duty free. When I called, she recognized the problem and assured me she would file an amended entry and arrange for me to be billed at the appropriate rate. There was no problem.

I received a past due notice from company headquarters for the $4,000 bill. When I called the local office, I discovered that the former manager quit and things are in turmoil. It required several calls to reach the new manager and most of the day for her to return with the news that all was well. Again.

I believe that all will be as it should. Nevertheless, this is a good example of why you should check your brokerage bills carefully and pursue any required corrections until they are accomplished. It is not enough for a staff member to tell you they WILL take care of the problem. Keep after them until the deed is done.

Prohibited and Restricted Items

Some of the things you are tempted to buy may be prohibited or restricted. Prohibited items include the products of endangered animals, such as ivory and the furs of large cats, and all products of countries the United States government does not like at the moment, such as cigars from Cuba. It is impossible to be absolutely certain what is or is not included. Use common sense and contact Customs for their booklet "Know Before You Go". If you have questions about a particular item contact Fish and Wildlife if it involves animals or the Customs specialist for that particular classification. They are usually helpful and informative.

Importing textiles almost always entails dealing with restrictions. Many times it involves the availability of "quota" for importation into the United States. Basically what this means is that the U.S. will allow only a fixed amount of textiles to be imported each year. This figure will change periodically as trade treaties are negotiated and renegotiated. You will probably not know for sure whether or not there is any quota available at the time you make your purchase unless you deal with someone in the country of origin that has connections necessary to receive a quota assignment. If you gamble on quota being available and are wrong your shipment can sit in a bonded warehouse for a very long time. This is true for commercial shipments but normally does not apply to several pieces for personal use. Check with the textile specialist and your customs broker before you go. If you consider importing weavings you should know as much about the quota status as possible, choose a country that is not restricted, or choose a fiber such as silk that as of this time can be freely imported. Be careful with textiles.

Gateway Cities

Many international flights to and from the United States originate or terminate in the gateway cities of New York, Miami, Houston, Dallas, Chicago, Los Angeles, San Francisco, or Seattle. Appendix 3 provides phone numbers for U.S. Customs and Fish and Wildlife in each city as well several customs brokers. Since I have not done business with all of these brokers this is not an endorsement of any of them. Talk with them and see if any are suitable. If you want more to choose from or if you are clearing customs elsewhere, consult the telephone yellow pages. Try your library for phone books from distant locations.

Rules and Shipping Abroad

Is it okay to bring it out of the country? The answer to this question is usually a resounding "Maybe."

Many of the items you want to buy are from the large grey area of antiques and semi-collectibles. It is not always easy to determine if they are legally allowed to be exported. It was suggested to me that the important thing is whether or not they normally check your bags before departure. While there is some validity to this point of view, there is always the possibility of a search. If you try to sneak out with something of importance the penalties can be very severe. They can include confiscation of your merchandise, fines, jail, whatever. Caveat smuggler.

An importer friend who manages to find truly magnificent antiques wherever he goes recently tried an exploratory trip to Mongolia. While unable to find the items he was looking for, he was able to buy an assortment of unusual textiles, weapons, and small collectibles. Strolling through Ulan Bator he found himself closely scrutinized by the police who took him to headquarters several times. They told him that he would not be able to leave with any of the things he had purchased. Local contacts verified this.

Not only would customs seize whatever they could find but they would also try to solicit as much as they could in the way of bribes. After the bribes were paid they would take everything anyway. It took a year and a lot of money before he successfully got everything to the U.S.

Most important is the practical way in which customs handles things. This is far more critical than what the official policy is, although the two are usually at least loosely interrelated. Finding where the line is drawn is a matter of testing and experience. The placement of the line will also depend on you. Your gender, ethnicity, appearance, the state of world politics, and the impression you make on the officials will all have a bearing on your results. Unfortunately, none of this does you any good in determining what is or is not allowable.

You have to start somewhere. Get in touch with the embassy or consulate of the countries you are going to be visiting. Addresses and telephone numbers for many countries are given in Appendix 2. If you can not find a listing there try directory assistance in New York or Washington, D.C. or contact the embassy of a country that has close ties to your target country. For example you would expect to get information about the former Soviet republics from the Russian Embassy.

Find out if there is a consulate in your city or one nearby. Consulates tend to be less formal. You may be able to form an acquaintanceship with someone there. Tell them what you are planning and ask them what problems there are in doing it. Be completely truthful. Hold nothing back. It is much better to find out that what you are planning is impossible before you waste time and money.

Ask if they have any suggestions on how to deal with the problems they foresee. They may give you suggestions or at least let you know what is going to be most troublesome.

You will probably hear something like "You can bring them out in non-commercial quantities" for most grey area items. If you try to get them to be more specific they often start stonewalling. As a group they are fairly noncommittal.

If you tell them point blank that you are considering making commercial sized shipments you may get a referral to a friend or family member in the shipping business in their country. The best way to utilize this information is to write a letter detailing your plans as specifically as possible. Ask if they can arrange for export clearance and shipping to the U.S. for the items you want. Fax them or use overseas express mail or a courier service like Federal Express. Ask for a prompt reply.

It may be difficult to get a conclusive answer about export requirements even after you arrive. Do not believe what dealers tell you about an item's exportability unless you have a relationship of trust with them.

You may want to visit the cultural ministry or customs office to get their opinion before you make a purchase. Make an appointment if you can. Otherwise stop by. Be prepared to wait awhile. Tell them what you want to do. Find out if there is perhaps a fee that may be paid for export documentation. This is not a suggestion that you offer a bribe. Some countries have stamp and documentation guidelines for exactly this sort of thing.

Meeting with customs seems like the logical choice to find out what you can do but it may be a waste of time. The actual experience you have will depend on the inspector you get. Talking with someone else may not yield you any practical information or binding guidelines. Still, it probably will not hurt to talk with them. The only bad result would be if it caused you to be targeted. This is probably paranoia, but maybe not.

You can also try to contact foreign shippers through the Chamber of Commerce in your destination cities. I have had remarkable success with letters simply addressed to "Chamber of Commerce" along with the city and country. I received replies from more places than not including Baghdad, Budapest, and Bogota. I request information about shipping companies and exporters who deal in the things I want to purchase.

You can wait until you arrive overseas and contact local friends or acquaintances for recommendations. Check with the U.S. embassy or consulate.

Shippers are obviously necessary for large items. If you are dealing with a very large shipment you should consider ocean freight. It can take quite a bit of time but the savings over air freight are substantial.

A local shipper may be able to cut through much of the red tape. In fact it is probable that a lot of the red tape you will encounter is placed there to keep these folks in business. If you buy and carry, they are cut out of the picture. You will usually be able to get straight answers from shippers about what can and cannot be done and what the charges will be. The grey area becomes more black and white. Some items that clearly reside in the black area may receive special dispensations if you find the right shipper. Be very specific about what you want done when you are making your inquiries. You may find someone who can help. If you are told that what you want to do cannot be done ask if there might be a different way to do it. Try to find alternatives.

Insure your shipments with an all risk policy. Unhappily this is not possible in some places and may be very expensive in others. I have shipped things without insurance but it is stressful and I do not recommend it. The shipper you select should be experienced and have an actual place of business. Having a regular table at the coffee shop does not count. Do not leave until you have a copy of the packing list which should list everything that is being shipped. Try to get an idea of when the shipment will be sent and approximately when you should be able to expect it. Tell the shipper you want the airbill number or ocean routing information faxed to you as soon as it is available. There will be a charge for this but it is worth it. When you begin to get worried you can use this information to track your shipment down.

Using a shipper can help clear export hurdles but it also puts more steps and people in the process. There are more things that can go wrong. Your circumstances will determine what you decide to do. While I have experienced delays and some breakage (less than 10%) on every shipment I've made, the overall results have been good.

Early in my importing career I decided that I needed to be able to deal with every aspect of the customs and shipping process. I was looking for hands on experience. For one of my projects I determined that I would make all of the necessary arrangements for shipping several hundred weavings by air freight from La Paz, Bolivia to my shop in Houston.

I arrived at the La Paz airport at around 9 AM with my boxes. The shipping manager at Lloyd Arero Boliviano spoke English and was very helpful. They would be happy to handle my shipment. All I needed to do was fill out a few forms.

The forms themselves were straightforward. I

quickly completed them and proudly displayed them to the manager. They looked just fine to him. Customs, however ,would need to approve them. The customs office was on the opposite end of the airport complex. It was about a twenty minute walk at the 11,000 feet altitude. No officials were around. The secretary thought they might return in time for the afternoon flights. I should come back then. She had no other suggestions.

I walked back to the air freight office. They had no suggestions. I went back at noon. No luck. Finally at 3 PM some uniforms began to show up. One of them spoke English. He said they could help me after they processed the flight that had just arrived. About forty-five minutes later he signed and stamped the forms without without asking me any questions.

I returned to the air freight office with my trophy, glad to be finished. I was greeted with the news that the narcotics police had to give their approval. They were located in the basement of the main terminal. He thought there was a fee. He did not know how much it was. I was feeling less than pleased with my decision to take care of everything myself.

When I got to the main terminal, no one seemed to know where I was supposed to go. A security officer who appeared to be surprised at my question finally gave me directions. I went downstairs and proceeded along a deserted hallway. I found the room number. There was no sign. I knocked softly. The door was opened by a small boy, perhaps nine or ten years old. I could see past him into the room.

There was a narrow iron bed, a cluttered desk, and a television tuned to cartoons.

"Policia Narcótica aquí?" I asked. "Sí" was the reply. They were returning in twenty minutes. I went back upstairs confused and concerned.

When I returned the boy was gone. At the desk was a small man who reminded me of a bull-fighter. He wore suit pants and a white shirt with the sleeves rolled up. Lounging on the bed engrossed in the cartoons was a caricature of a B movie prison guard in uniform. I wasn't happy. Neither of them spoke English. I showed them the forms. The thin man took them and asked me some questions about what I was shipping. I answered him as well as I could. He smiled and said there was no problem as he signed and stamped the forms. There would however be a stamp fee. The large man stood up. Here comes the shakedown, I thought. The entire amount was less than two dollars. They were concerned that they did not have the correct change to give me.

I made it back to the air freight office shortly before 5 PM and the rest of the procedure went smoothly. The day's tensions were brought on by problems more imagined than real, but it was easy to see that things could have turned out less pleasantly. I wasted quite a bit of time. This was my last attempt at arranging air freight from another country. I now either bring it back as luggage or use a shipper. They not only take care of local details efficiently, they do it relatively inexpensively.

At the Airport

Never try to carry a prohibited item through customs. The stakes are too high. You will have enough problems with grey area objects.

Arrive at the airport early. Very early. If something goes wrong there may be time to do something about it. For example, if a large part of your shipment is not allowed to leave with you, it might possible to talk them into letting you leave it with a local friend or even a dealer you trust. Maybe you could check it at the hotel where you stayed. You might be able to salvage something. Perhaps you could arrange to have it shipped later. Maybe you could figure out another way to get it out. The inspector might even decide to let you slip through this time when he realizes that you have alternatives. Anything is better than having it confiscated. If that happens it is gone for good.

Your attitude will have a lot to do with how inspectors deal with you. If you appear to be scared or shifty expect them to spend a lot of time with you and your luggage.

Intelligent. Confident, but not arrogant. Friendly and open. Perhaps tired and a bit bored. These are the poses to strive for. If you can assume them properly you can cut down the chances of an extensive examination considerably. This is beneficial even if you have nothing to hide. Nothing good can come from conjuring up the interest of a customs inspector. Nothing. At the very least the efforts you make to carefully pack everything will be wasted.

If your baggage is selected for inspection, try to remain calm. Appearing to be nervous or irritated is definitely not recommended. Be polite and responsive. Do not try to engage the inspector in conversation. Do not volunteer anything. Have all of your travel documents in hand including currency exchange receipts, invoices, etc.

Rehearse what you plan to say about the items you have purchased. Where you bought them. How much you paid. What you think they are. Your complete story. This is especially important regarding the gray area items. If you practice what you are going to say you will sound more confident. If you sound confident it will go better for you.

Never ask if there is a problem, even if they make funny faces and chatter among themselves. Always act like everything is just fine. If the inspector begins to question you about something particular, politely but forcefully stand up for your position. Consider asking to speak to a supervisor if you feel your position is a valid one and the inspector is unyielding. If you feel strongly that money would do the trick and the item in question is important to you,you can ask," Is there a fee for this? I would like to take it with me if it is not too expensive." Do not be quick to do this. Do not encourage the solicitation of bribes or extra fees. Payments such as these are almost never necessary. Even if they want a tip you can probably get by without paying it if you are not doing something that violates regulations. If you are in violation, offering to make a payment may not help you anyway. If he is upset by your offer, apologize and back off immediately.

Just an observation. The area of your luggage that receives the most scrutiny is at the bottom around the edges. Side pockets and end pockets are also very popular. The space slightly to the left or right of center about a third of the way down does not get a lot of attention.

Your carry-on luggage will be looked at more closely than that which is checked through. Try to keep from having bulky or metallic pieces in it. You do not want to call attention to yourself.

Most of your airport experiences will end up being completely successful. Unfortunately, you will go through a fair amount of stress along the way. Try to stay relaxed. Breathe slowly and deeply and concentrate on your breaths while you are waiting. Take the process a step at a time. It will be over sooner than you think.

Chapter 11
Profits Here and There

As with most endeavors, your success depends on a combination of the skills you bring to the game, timing, and the smiles or frowns of the Goddess of Fortune.

Basic Business

If you have little previous business experience you will benefit from reading some of the books about starting and running small businesses. Select a book that discusses topics that you have questions about or that has some similarities to what you are considering.

You do not necessarily need a lot of money to start. The possibility of beginning a business like this with a small bankroll is one of the attractions. Of course, the more you have the better. Borrowing, especially in the early stages of your venture, is a bad idea. It takes away your independence and adds to stress and pressure.

The form of your business is determined by the number of people involved, tax considerations, financing, and liability concerns. A sole proprietorship offers the most flexibility and control; a corporation is more complicated and restrictive, but offers the best protection of your personal assets. Partnerships offer some of the best and worst of the other forms. Discuss your situation with your legal and tax professionals. Learn enough about what is involved in making these choices so that your time with the professionals is spent determining the answers to specific questions rather than planning your business.

Taxes, licenses, and other red tape are realities of doing business wherever you are. Discuss your plans with the appropriate professionals, although you can get some information from official sources or organizations like the Chamber of Commerce.

Focused Marketing

Buying right and selecting effective selling strategies are the most important things you can do to tilt the scales of success in your favor. Previous chapters have examined techniques for finding and buying merchandise; this chapter will primarily look at selling and the entire marketing process.

The importance of a narrow focus is a marketing decision that has its roots in the buying process. At first glance it does not seem to be logical. Simply stated, you will do your best if you concentrate as narrowly and as intently as possible. The natural tendency is to buy and sell as many things as you can. This is not normally the best strategy. Even when you have rationalized that you have encountered one of the exceptions to this rule, you will usually be wrong. This has been proven to me in practice many more times than I would care to discuss. If you are interested in some of the theory of focused marketing as well as some illustrations of failures and achievements by household name corporations, read <u>Bottom-Up Marketing</u> by Al Ries and Jack Trout published 1989 by McGraw-Hill (ISBN 0-07-052733-4). Even if you don't think you are interested, you should probably read it anyway.

The above concept of narrow focus will be true for 99% of those who read this book. There are, however, a few very agile participants in these markets who have the ability to surf the edge. They go from one hot zone to another with the greatest of ease, making money from whatever is currently in vogue. If you are enticed to succumb to this temptation, remember that your timing will have to be just about perfect. If you stay too long you may have all your money tied up in worthless stock when the music stops for the latest fad. That can put you out of business.

Plan your marketing strategy thoroughly before you begin. Determine who your potential customers are. How will you contact them? Where will you sell to them? What will your margins need to be?

Common sense coupled with your research may push you in the direction of your potential customers. But, it may not. Sometimes it is difficult to find the end user of your product. You want to get as close to the end user as possible. The more layers of "tweeners" or middlemen you bypass the more money you will make. More importantly, you will have greater control of your business and will not depend on others along the chain.

Contacting potential customers can be even more difficult. Analyze your best customers or those who you believe would make good customers. How did you come into contact with them? How do they choose what to buy and who do they buy from? What do they read? Where do they go? What can you do to make it desirable for them to buy from you? These are very complicated questions. Sometimes they have no good answer. You may not be able to reach them with anything you are thinking of doing. In some cases you may not be able to reach them at all. Even worse, you may spend a lot of time and money before you figure this out.

Flea Markets

As perplexing as this all may be, you have to begin somewhere. For many, the flea market setting is as good a place to sell as it is to buy. There is little red tape and it is cheap. It is a great place to test your products and ideas.

Before you set up, evaluate the spaces and displays that

catch your eye in a positive way. Figure out what it is about them that you like. How can you incorporate the obvious high points into your booth design?

You will usually have to take whatever space happens to be vacant. If you have a choice, try to get something to the right of the entrance near the front.

If the market is outdoors, invest in a quality canopy to protect you and your customers from the elements. Copeland Canopies of Santa Fe supplies many of the vendors at Trader Jack's Flea Market with canopies and display materials. Their number is 800-304-7578. They have a catalog and offer service by mail. Have chairs available for prospective customers to make themselves comfortable. Consider having iced tea or water available for them also.

Spend money on quality display materials. Most cities have display or exhibit service companies listed in the telephone yellow pages. You do not need custom made cases or materials to begin with, but the better your merchandise looks the better you will do. When making your display selections you should also be concerned with the security they afford, how well they travel, and how durable they are.

Do as much as is practically possible to delineate your space, to make it separate from what is around you. Sometimes the only effort that you can make is in the configuration of your displays. Potential customers need to be able to look at them without making a commitment. Your display should be inviting them into the area that is definitively yours.

The flea market atmosphere is the least secure of all of the places you will be considering. You cannot control who comes to your space and you can only control the space itself through the selection and organization of your display materials. You will experience some shoplifting. Try to minimize your losses. Secure your most valuable pieces. Consider only displaying a small sample of your best pieces. You can bring out additional treasures when you have a qualified buyer. Watch out for distractions and groups that seem to envelop your area. Be wary of large bags. If you feel uncomfortable about something that someone is doing, tell them to stop or to please put your merchandise down. You do not have to be distrustful of everyone; you do need to be vigilant.

Make use of professional looking signs, banners, and the like to give as much information about your product as possible. This saves you from answering repetitive questions. It also keeps potential customers interested and occupied when you are busy with someone else. It also makes it easier to establish rapport through this unspoken communication.

Have descriptive flyers available if they seem at all applicable. They almost always will be. At the very least have your business cards prominently displayed.

While not every product is suitable for flea market distribution, keep it in mind as a place where you can test out new ideas, prospect for new customers, and supplement other marketing strategies you are exploring. All of this plus the chance you may make quite a bit of money there!

Organized Trade and Collectible Shows

One time or periodic shows have many similarities to flea markets. The major difference is that they always cost significantly more. They may or may not have correspondingly more interested and qualified buyers. They will usually have much stiffer competition. As with many things, the past has probably seen the best of them.

Entrepreneurial vendors as well as other opportunistic observers correctly reasoned that it is much more profitable to run a show than participate in one. Pay no attention to the protestations of show promoters to the contrary. This is a very profitable business. In many areas the shows have expanded to the point where it is difficult for anyone other than the promoters to do well. This occurs both because of the number of shows that are promoted and the number of participants who exhibit at each show. As they grow proportionately beyond the numbers of buyers, things begin to unravel. If you have great stuff or great prices (preferably both) you can still make money if you are selective. At their best the shows give you exposure to a large number of potential customers that you might otherwise not meet. At their worst they disrupt some of the other promotional efforts you make.

Location is more important at organized shows than at flea markets. This is because there is more competition. You want to be in the main building, on the main floor, on the right, in front, on a corner. Your relative position can easily make the difference between a great show and a disaster.

As a first time vendor you will be faced with the Catch 22 of only securing a good space if the show is unproven or unproductive. The only way around this at a good show is to try to get to know the show promoters and convince them of the uniqueness of your product and the class it will add to their production. They have heard these types of tales many times before and you will probably not be successful. But, if you are actually bringing something new or unusual, you may have a chance of improving your space assignment. It also helps to apply early with a professional looking presentation package that describes you and your merchandise (photographs and references are especially good). Offering to pay in full far in advance may help move you to the front of the pack.

Some of the shows that give your product the best exposure are the New York Boutique, Fashion Accessories Expo, and Gift Shows; the Los Angeles Gift Show; the Ethnographic Show in Santa Fe; and the February Gem and Mineral Shows in Tucson. There are other similar types of shows that would be more appropriate if your product does not easily fit into any of these categories. None of these shows are inexpensive. Attend one as an observer before committing yourself to participation.

Setting Prices

Pricing is an important part of marketing strategy. In organized shows where competition is at its most intense, relative pricing is something that you need to spend a lot of time thinking about. Will you give discounts for volume purchases? If so, how much and when? Are these guidelines concrete or flexible?

If a competitor is selling a similar item for less, will you match his price? What if he lowers his again? What if he is obviously dumping his stock? Price wars are not good for business. Sometimes it is better not to compete; other times you will have to. You can't allow your competitor to make all of the sales because he is selling for a little less. On the other hand, he may have done a better job of buying than you. The more focused you are in your buying the less you will be faced with these troubling confrontations.

Pricing your merchandise correctly is difficult even when your competition is not your main concern. Price your merchandise high enough to make a reasonable profit without encouraging new competitors to come into the market or to make yourself vulnerable to price undercutting by the ones who are already there.

It is sometimes advantageous to set a high price on your merchandise. This is especially true if you deal in one of a kind pieces or original works of art. In addition to increasing your profit margins you may also create an air of exclusivity and quality. Joy perfume and Rolls Royce are two good examples of this effect.

It can be perplexing to set your initial price. What should your markup be? Many importers begin with the idea that they would like to double their in hand cost. (The in hand cost is the cost of the product at its origin plus all of the expense of getting it to your base of operation.) They then shift upward or downward based on their perceived value of the item, what competitors are charging for similar items, the expenses necessary to market the item, and whether they are selling a few or many units at a time. Aside from the idea of doubling your in hand cost, evaluate the market and determine what works. Sometimes a markup of 10% is more than enough and other times getting 300% of your in hand cost is not nearly enough.

An acquaintance of mine, the young scion of a multi-generational Italian trading family, set out on his own to deal in antique furniture and decorative accessories from India. With a good eye and natural flair for the business, he selected a collection of outstanding unusual pieces. He shipped container loads to a warehouse space in New York City.

Almost everyone who saw his selections was impressed with them, but sales were disappointing. The reason? Without exception he was told that the prices were simply too high to leave any room for profit for the purchaser, especially after the cost of shipping to their location was added in. It appeared that little could be done. Due to substantial warehouse expenses and anemic sales, his pricing strategy of doubling his in hand cost resulted in significant losses.

He took radical action. The warehouse was closed. The best of the pieces were moved to a small showroom and the rest were sold off at bargain basement prices. On his next trip to India he took extensive videos of the best pieces he came across. He personalized and sent these video catalogues to the potential customers who had balked at his prices. The following proposition was made. He would arrange purchase of the items they wanted for a fee of 10% of the purchase price with a $1,000 minimum. The merchandise would be sent to them freight collect with payment to be made by sight draft. (With a sight draft, the documents necessary to clear customs are sent to you at a local bank. You pay the amount of the invoice and the documents are released to you for customs clearance. While some trust is involved, the bill of lading or shipping invoice must match the cargo received. An inspection by an independent third party can be specified in the agreement, if necessary.)

With his new finders fee method of doing business both profits and sales went up spectacularly. He was also able to take money out of his business, since much less stock on hand was required.

___

How could tripling your money not be enough? I have a personal example from the Andean textile market.

Some years ago I traveled throughout South America looking for old silver crosses. Occasionally, I would buy antique weavings. When I bought them, I would usually buy ten or twenty pieces at a time at a common price per piece. Some of the weavings were of obviously better quality because of color, age, condition, or design. If I priced them all the same, the best would sell and I would be left with the dregs. Consequently, I ranged my prices from about 50% over my in hand cost to 500% over for the very best pieces. They sold at a consistent rate throughout the entire range.

I eventually got hooked on these weavings and amassed a collection of several hundred. As my business became focused on antique beads and unusual components for jewelry design I made little effort to sell these textiles. Several years after I stopped traveling in South America at least one of the Andean countries prohibited the export of any weavings made in the 1950's or before. If I decide to sell my collection, it will be at a higher price than before. This is not because I revel in price gouging. It is because these pieces have become irreplaceable. If you do less when you find yourself in this fortunate situation, you will regret it.

Discounts

After a base price is determined discounts, if any, are usually based on the volume which is purchased. Lots of people will ask you for discounts. Only consider giving them based on purchases that are being made at that time. Virtually no one who has wheedled a discount from me on the basis of promised future business has become a substantial customer. This is true even when these people seemed to exhibit the appropriate characteristics. It is a well practiced buying ploy to guard against. If your pricing and discount policy is well founded there is little reason to deviate from it. Almost every time you do, you will only succeed in selling your product for less without receiving the compensating larger amount of business.

Selling

In many ways selling is much easier than buying. You know how much you have paid for your merchandise and what your expenses are. Once you have developed a pricing policy, most of the information you need to make an intelligent and profitable transaction will be at your fingertips. Contrast this to many buying situations where much of what you need to know to make a good deal may initially be hidden from you.

Most of your transactions will be buyer driven. You will not be talking people into purchasing something that they really do not want. You have the greatest opportunity to influence the sale by making potential customers feel good about buying from you and buying the item they are considering. Knowledge of your product and honesty in your discussion and dealings will do you the most good. These tactics will help build long term relationships and will reward you with the business of large knowledgeable customers. These large customers, who may make up as little as 5% of your numerical total, could be responsible for 80% or more of your business.

Publicity and Advertising

When you are operating solely within the confines of the markets and bazaars there is little reason for you to advertise or worry a lot about getting your message out to the public. Your location and displays are the most important parts of your marketing plan. This is also true if you are participating in organized shows.

As you include fixed locations or mail order in your strategy you need to be much more concerned about contacting potential customers. This is where publicity and advertising are important.

For the sake of simplicity we will consider publicity as non paid information about you or your product that is publicly broadcast through print or over the airways. It also means being presented as something that is newsworthy. This feature makes publicity many times more valuable than the same amount of exposure in a paid advertising format. Someone besides you thinks that you or your product is important. This is why publicists are paid hefty sums to get products and personalities mentioned favorably.

You will probably be your own publicist. In this role you will identify likely candidates to spread your message. This includes local newspapers, radio stations, magazines, and television stations. If it is appropriate, you can explore these same sources on the regional or national level.

You then need to figure out how to make your situation newsworthy and appealing. Identify writers, broadcasters, sections, columns, or programs that are compatible with your story. Pay attention to the style and context in which their reports appear. Structure your proposal within these guidelines. Find out who makes the decisions for story selection and submit the best proposal or news release that you possibly can. It may be productive to follow up your written submission with a phone call or request for an appointment.

Your proposal or release should be as interesting and informative as possible. There should be a hook to grab attention, to make what you are doing look unique and entertaining. Include photos or a video if you can put together a quality piece. Make it easy for them to contact you.

If you find someone that gives you exposure once, it is likely that they will do so again. This is not a one way street. While you are getting something valuable, remember that the job of your contact is at least in part to find interesting stories like yours. Developing a complementary relationship can result in continuing benefits for both of you.

You will put in a lot of work prospecting for publicity. It will also cost you some money to prepare a professional looking presentation. No matter how much you spend on your publicity campaign, you can be sure that you are getting better value than for money spent on paid advertising. Exhaust all of your reasonable possibilities for getting publicity before you consider talking to anyone about buying advertising space.

Small businesses probably spend more money unwisely on advertising and related non-necessities such as logo design, special business cards, and custom printing than in any other area. These look pretties can do a lot to improve the owner's image of his business, but often do little to help the bottom line.

Whatever money is spent on individual promotion related items should be part of an overall marketing strategy. This strategy should be well thought out with specific goals in mind. As a practical consideration you should never consider an advertising salesperson's cold call pitch to sell you space. Decide where, how, and most importantly why you want to buy advertising space and then make your appointments with the appropriate media representatives.

To be most effective your advertising should be strongly focused. If you are promoting a store or gallery location your focus will be geographic. One type of publication that can be effective in getting out your message is the city or regional magazine. The type referred to here combines editorial coverage with art, movie, and music news as opposed to the advertising only papers. These are also good bets for free publicity if you approach them properly.

Promotion that Pays

You can even make money promoting yourself and your business. Write an article, teach a class at the local community college or leisure learning organization, or put together a seminar on your area of expertise. These can also be done without payment. The benefits are considerable. First,you begin to establish yourself as an expert. You also come into contact with people who have by their participation indicated an interest in what you are doing. In the case of written material make sure that those who read your article have a way to contact you.

At Home by Appointment

Selling your goods from home has an obvious advantage of being inexpensive. It has been used by private art and antique dealers for years. Privacy for both you and your customers is another plus. The major downsides are lack of exposure and possible security problems.

The home showroom is only practical if you have some effective forms of attracting customers. In most cases it is used to conduct business with prospective buyers you meet at shows or who respond to your advertising.

The showroom area should be separate from your actual living area and well secured. This includes a monitored security system with a panic button feature and lockable, good quality storage facilities. Do not meet with customers alone. Pre-qualify first time contacts as to the general suitability of your merchandise and prices before making an appointment. Be especially wary of unknown callers who seem like potential buyers but whose questions are different than those you usually get.

Warehouse/Office

A warehouse setting usually houses large items such as furniture and architectural antiques, but can be used for any type of product. It is similar to the home showroom in that you will seldom enjoy any walkby customers. If you are lucky your warehouse area will experience an avant garde renovation and you will have gallery space for storage room rent.

If your business is working, consider buying your building. You not only guard against inevitable rent increases but also build up real estate equity rather than a stack of rent receipts. There may be other factors such as the question of flexibility, large down payments, and possible increased liability to think about, but at least look into it.

Gallery/Shop

A gallery space in a shopping area offers the most walk by traffic exposure for your business. If you are not sure that the space you are considering will accomplish this, do not get it. The costs of operating even a simple storefront can be enormous. Only when you are fully committed and in the midst of it will all the costs become apparent. This is true even if you are sure that you have thought of everything. You will find yourself spending far too much time at the end of each day writing checks to people you never imagined would have any contact with your business.

It is impossible to put too much emphasis on the location of any space which you are considering. It is a much more common mistake to lease space that is OK and looks cheap than to lease space that is obviously good but expensive. If you are going to take a shot at the retail side of the game it is better to go for the best space possible even if it looks expensive. The reason is simple. It is often impossible to spend enough in advertising to get the same traffic in a less costly space. If you can't make yourself go for the expensive high traffic location, you may want to reconsider your thoughts about opening a shop.

Another harsh reality... Even if you lease what appears to be the golden location you may not make it. This is a very bad situation to be in. You not only have spent money on build out and fixtures but perhaps were introduced to the very strange concept of key money (essentially extra money you give the landlord in addition to the amount called for in your lease for which you receive nothing other than the pleasure of paying him large sums of rent each month). You probably signed a long term lease for which you are still liable. Try to negotiate an escape clause up front that allows you to cancel the lease for a fixed payment. If you can do this it will usually be on a sliding scale based on the time left on the lease. It costs about one month's rent per year remaining at the time the lease is canceled.

These are not pleasant thoughts but they are some of the things you may have to deal with. Others include neverending escalating rent increases and paying a percentage of your gross to the man with the big set of keys. (This is not to suggest that landlords are taking advantage of their tenants. It is just that they hold all the cards when it comes to leasing prime properties. Perhaps this is as it should be. The purchase and the development of the prime property did not come cheaply to them and they should rightly expect a good return on their investment.)

The best way around this is to buy your own building. Try to negotiate a lease purchase. This gives you some time to see how things are going before you take the final plunge. You will find it profitable to scout for locations that are prime for your business but not necessarily prime for other businesses. This gives you a great location at a less than prime rent or purchase price. Older areas of a city that are redeveloping are often worth visiting. Remember that even here, perhaps especially here, you want to get the best location you possibly can. One of the best illustrations of this is the Soho area of Manhattan where one block can be the difference between upscale shopping and rat infested tenements.

Unless you have an unquenchable sense of adventure or are actually a real estate speculator in disguise, you do not want to be one of the first to try to reclaim one of these urban areas. You might do really well, but you should also keep in mind that pioneers are often the guys who end up with arrows in their backs.

Pick your location along the logical traffic lines of existing businesses or attractions that draw in the type of people you want to have in your store. The more attractions the better. Make certain that the crowds actually have to walk by your store. NOT CLOSE. DIRECTLY IN FRONT OF YOUR ENTRANCE!!!

Hours

The hours you are open are always important and may make the difference between being successful and going under. A quick personal example... My shop in Houston was located in an old but well renovated art deco shopping center. My hours were from 11 AM-8 PM Sunday-Thursday and 11 AM-10 PM Friday and Saturday. Many of the neighboring shops were open from 10 AM-5 PM. While the center appeared to be a fairly upscale walk around shopping area it was in reality a collection of destination locations. That is, there was not nearly as much crossover or window shopping as you might have expected. This changed in the evening due to high traffic at several popular restaurants and an independent/international type movie theater. The fact that my shop prospered, while many of my neighbors failed to live through their first lease was directly related to the difference in our hours. They were open when they wanted to be open; I was open when the crowds were there.

Employees

Initially your staff will be you. The way you decide to choose additional help will affect the success of your business. Your customers want to deal with you if they can. The next best thing for them is to deal with someone who shares their appreciation for your merchandise. Candidates that fit this description can frequently be found by prospecting your existing customers. They already have somewhat of a knowledge of your product and may be interested in receiving some of their pay in merchandise.

No matter how carefully you select your employees you will eventually experience theft or some other serious problems with them. You will also get virtually no help in this regard from any of the law enforcement authorities you contact. You may even find yourself in a position of legal jeopardy depending on how you choose to handle these situations. It pays to consult a lawyer who is experienced in employment law before you act. Be careful.

A key element in your relationship with your employees is that they know what is expected of them. Give all new employees a written summary of your policies regarding working hours, duties, missed shifts, dealing with customers, and handling other situations or possible problems. If you are feeling legalistic, have them sign a statement that they read these guidelines.

The following employee manual was given to all new employees at my ethnographic gallery in Houston. They were designed to meet the specific needs of that business. While they may give you some useful ideas, you should recognize that your requirements will most likely differ from mine.

EMPLOYEE MANUAL

1. **TIME CARDS** Do not fill out time cards at the beginning of the time period for the entire pay period. Fill them out daily. If you get here late, write it down. If you stay late, write it down.

2. **ATTIRE** Casual but nice. Walking shorts okay. Short shorts and old jeans not o.k.

3. **TIME OFF** If you need a day off, talk to Christina and arrange for someone to cover your shift. You are responsible for finding a substitute.

4. **SALES SLIPS**
   Write down items and amount - i.e. gold and tourmaline ring not just ring.
   Subtotal and add tax USE THE ADDING MACHINE WE ALL MAKE MISTAKES
   For tax exempt purchases, make sure the tax number is on file or it must be written on top of the sales slip and a tax form filled out. The blank tax forms are next to the radio in a manila envelope.
   Sales Date
   Note form of payment—Cash, Check (including number), MasterCard, Visa, American Express, Gift Certificate, Store credit, Travelers' Check
   Initial the sales slip
   Get their name if possible - from all checks and charge slips

5. DISCOUNTS

Never offer a discount! If they ask and the purchase is over $100 you can give up to 15% off with cash or check only

15% discount on cash or check purchases <u>ONLY</u>

If absolutely necessary, Amex can be discounted 10% and MasterCard or Visa can be discounted 11%. ONLY if necessary.

Take the discount before adding tax

Wholesale bead discount 30% off at $300 or to existing wholesale bead customers or people who mention *Ornament* ad. This is a loose bead discount only. If they want a discount on other merchandise and above criteria fit they can have 15%.off.

6. CHECKS

Make sure that the amount is correct and that the written and numeric amounts match. NO checks for over the amount of purchase

Check Date. No post-dated checks.

Check address against drivers license—get current address.

Initial check and write drivers license on it.

Get daytime phone number.

Make sure that the check is signed.

7. CREDIT CARDS

Check Expiration Date. LOOK AT CARD!

Imprint—<u>Make sure you use the correct form</u> (American Express or MasterCard/Visa)

Write down date of charge

Fill in all sections: Detail, Sub-total, Tax & Total

Get Approval Code

Initial Slip

Note whether the Card is a MasterCard or Visa if appropriate.

Ask for daytime phone number

Get Signature

—If the code Call Center appears—
Dial the appropriate telephone number posted on the index card on the wall; tell the operator that you need an approval code. They will ask for the information on the index card plus the card number, expiration date and amount. Hold on for the approval code.

8. LAYAWAY
20% down and 90 days to pay
Use a separate form for EACH item.
Use form in layaway file. Fill out <u>ALL</u> areas.
Fill out one sales slip with the purchasers name and address to be placed with the item in the back. Write down—what the item is, the amount, tax and down payment along with the date.
Fill out a second sales slip as a receipt for the amount of the down payment. Write down what item the down payment is for.

9. LAYAWAY PAYMENTS
Record payment both in the file up front and on the sales slip on the item in back.
On the receipt for the payment write down what it is a payment for.
If it is a final payment attach the form from the file to our copy of the sales receipt.

10. STORE CREDIT
On a sales slip write the person's name and the amount of the credit. If it is a gift certificate, include the name of the purchaser and the recipient. If it is a return,note amount and tax separately as they appear on the original sales slip.
A gift certificate receipt (to the person buying the certificate) either needs to have the tax added on, or tax must be backed out of the amount on the store credit.
When someone comes in and wishes to use their store credit, subtract the amount not including tax from the

total before tax.

11. ON APPROVAL

In order to take a rug or textile out on approval, the person must leave with us either a signed credit card slip or check for the full amount of the piece. If it is a credit card slip, get an approval code just as if the sale were going through then. Pieces should not be taken out for longer than 48 hours. Get a firm return date and let the person know that if the piece is not back by then their check or credit card voucher will be deposited.

12. RETURNS and REFUNDS

Gifts:

Exchange or store credit within 90 days of purchase.

Ask who purchased the gift and the approximate date so we can find our copy of the receipt. The receipts are stored by date in the expandable file below the counter. Use the receipt to determine the exchange value.

If you can't find the receipt, but they brought in the gift box with the Lost Cities sticker, give them credit if you can determine the exchange value.

If you can't resolve the situation using these guide lines, get their phone number and Christina will contact them. Write a brief note describing the problem.

Exchange or credit requests (excluding gifts):

If they have their receipt or you can find it in the file, give them an exchange or credit within 90 days of the purchase date.

For special situations or problems, get the phone number and Christina will contact them. Write a brief note describing the problem. Notify Christina if the person making the request has made previous exchanges.

Broken items:

If we can fix it or restring it we will do it at no charge.

If we can't fix it we will replace it or give them a store credit within 90 days of the purchase if they have their copy of the receipt or we can find ours.

For special situations or problems,get the phone number and Christina will contact them. Write a brief note describing the problem.

Refunds:

If the customer insists on a refund rather than exchange or store credit, they need to give you their copy of the receipt within 30 days of the purchase date. We will credit their credit card account if the purchase was made by credit card. We will refund cash purchases or check purchases (only after we are sure that the check has cleared-10 days) by check. Christina or Michelle can process the refunds.

For special situations or problems get their phone number and Christina will contact them. Write a brief note describing the problem.

OPENING PROCEDURES

Unlock Door
Turn off alarm - always carry card w/code in case of error
Turn on lights
Turn on a/c
Unlock gates - put open sign in window
Turn on music (Play all cd's in their numerical order)
Rinse out and refill coffee pot with water
Clean/Dust all cases and counters
Count drawer

CLOSING PROCEDURES

Close and lock door
Sign off and out of window/close and lock gates

Ring checklist
Tally receipts and balance drawer
Put receipts and money in bottom right hand of desk in
   back
Unplug coffeepot
Turn off radio, lights and a/c (turn to 80 in summer & 60
   in winter)
Set alarm
Lock door from outside

A step by step training process guides the new employee through all of their tasks. Both written and verbal descriptions of your merchandise enable them to deal with the questions of prospective buyers. Explain all new merchandise to everyone. Do not assume anything is obvious or that they will just pick it up.

During their orientation, all new employees of my ethnographic gallery were introduced to the pieces in each case as well as those hung on the walls or stacked on the floor. Almost all of the pieces were labeled with descriptive tags. For further information the new employees were referred to a more detailed merchandise information booklet which was updated periodically. They were encouraged to take a copy home with them. A few excerpts follow.

Silks

Sarongs. Handwoven silks; mostly vegetable dyes. Ikat process where threads are tie-dyed before being woven. The design is in the threads before it is woven. The process is called *Mat-mi*. Most of these pieces were woven before 1940. After 1946 most silks in Thailand were woven by machine and used chemical dyes. These sarongs were made in the northeast part of Thailand along the border with Laos in Udon Thani.

Loom Parts

These are antique loom parts from the Akha tribe in Northern Thailand. They have had a small brace added recently to make them usable for hanging decorative weavings. They are pictured on page 284 of Peoples of the Golden Triangle.

Rugs

Tibetan All of our Tibetan rugs were made before the Chinese invasion of Tibet in 1959. These pre-occupation pieces were made with wool gathered in areas over 11,000 feet. Wool from animals raised at this height has a high lanolin content. The high lanolin content makes the rugs softer and fluffier when compared to those made by Tibetan refugees today with lowland wool.

Boxes

Khmer Silver. Little silver betel nut boxes. Some shaped like animals.

Wooden boxes and bowls. Rajasthan, north central India. mid to late 19th century. Mostly rosewood. Dark pieces are mahogany.

Porcelain. Chinese. Traded throughout Southeast Asia. All of ours were purchased in Jakarta.

In addition to this merchandise description booklet, which eventually grew to over 50 pages, there were over 100 books on different areas of ethnographic art, textiles, and jewelry available as references for both employees and customers.

You may want to use several part time workers rather than one or two full time employees. It can save you money on required benefits and makes scheduling less challenging. You are in a stronger position when dealing with your personnel and it is it less likely that you will be held up by them at crucial times.

The greatest benefit of having a shop or gallery space is that you have complete control over the setting and atmosphere. The layout, means of display, music and general style are all important components. Consider the effect that each will have on your sales environment. Ideally the ambiance you create will irresistibly attract potential customers while causing those who have no real buying interest to go on their way without wasting too much of your time.

Rotate your merchandise throughout the store. Frequently both customers and employees alike asked me when the new shipment came in after I did some major rearranging.

The more unique your merchandise is the less pressure you will feel on your prices. If you notice other stores carrying an item similar to yours consider phasing it out, especially if it is not high volume or high margin. You may decide to continue carrying it but you should at least think about the alternative. This will keep your merchandise fresh and will help keep you from getting involved in price wars.

Problem Situations

No matter what form your business takes, you will deal with unpleasant people and situations. In retail these encounters are more frequent. Some of them will be your fault, some will be the result of misunderstandings, others will be caused by people trying to take advantage of you. Handling these problems goes more smoothly if you have a predetermined policy for dealing with them. It helps if you write them out. Include returns, repairs, credit (best left to be handled by MasterCard, Visa, and American Express, and banks), approvals, exchanges, trades, etc.

If you are at fault, the best solution is to do whatever is reasonable to make it right. Take this approach even if there is some doubt about your culpability. If you feel the customer is trying to take unfair advantage, you still may want to try to make them happy. Nordstrom's built a great reputation of dealing with problems in this manner. However, you are not Nordstrom's. Sharp angle shooters (these range from society matrons to the guys in seersucker suits and alligator shoes) seem to take aim more directly at small businesses. Do not allow anyone to talk you into doing something you feel uncomfortable about just because they have an intimidating persona or spout promises of large deals.

Now for a few tales from the real world of retail.

---

(1) Less than a month after I opened my shop, a friendly, well dressed woman appeared on a busy Friday night. As she went from case to case, she exclaimed over and over again how much she loved everything we had. Where had we been all of her life? She bought over $1000 worth of jewelry which she paid for by check. She also asked me to hold about twice that much for a few days that she wanted to think about. Her sale was the largest I had made in my short career, so I gladly did as she asked. She was supposed to come in by the following Tuesday.

Late Tuesday afternoon she called and asked if I could hold her selections for a bit longer. Friday evening she came in and over the course of several hours she spent about twice as much as she had on her first visit. I was thrilled.

Almost three months later a woman who identified herself as the secretary of my big customer entered the store and asked to speak with me. Her boss wanted to return some of the items she had purchased, she said. When I asked her how much was involved and what the problem was it took her awhile to get around to it. When she finally did, the proposed return totaled about 75% of the purchase. No real reason was given. She simply wanted her money back.

(2) The son of a customer had made career choices which resulted in several trips to the penitentiary. While out on parole he became enamored with one of my employees who happened to be married. He began leaving flowers for her and asking lots of questions about her. When told of her marital status he said that he just wanted to be friends. His therapist felt that it would be beneficial for him to learn to relate to women.

(3) A couple walked into the shop late Friday evening and announced that they wanted to buy the entire front window which contained a collection of antique weavings. The total was over $5000. They wanted to pay with an out of state check.

(4) On several occasions aggressive panhandlers set up next to my doorway and began accosting passers-by. Many potential browsers avoided them by walking across the street. Those who braved the gauntlet complained or

entered with pained expressions on their faces.

(5) I hired a personable young woman who had been a regular customer. Almost from the beginning the cash drawer came up short on her shifts. She would smile, apologize ,and appear confused when I discussed this with her. Merchandise began to disappear. First small inexpensive items. Eventually an expensive sapphire ring set in 18 karat gold.

(6) A pair of drunks stumbled into the shop brandishing a bottle of wine. They wanted to know if I had a corkscrew. (Apparently the bottle they boosted did not have a screw cap.)

(7) On Friday or Saturday night, during one of the rushes we experienced when the nearby movie let out, I could expect the arrival of a wealthy former art dealer. In she would come with chauffeur in tow. Depending on the state of her medication she would quiz me for an hour or more about my collection or walk from case to case mumbling to herself. During her more lucid moments she tried to convince me to trade my antique beads and silver for her wonderful jewelry creations or pieces of new looking pottery which she insisted was pre-Hispanic. She often brought samples along which she loudly described for one and all.

What would you do in these situations? With hindsight I could certainly improve on some of my choices. Here is what happened.

(1) The lady who wanted to return almost everything was never available for direct discussion. Dealing through her secretary we finally agreed that she would return about half of what she purchased and keep the other half. Later I learned that this woman was solely responsible for changing the liberal return policy of a nearby contemporary jewelry gallery to that of "All sales are final".

(2) I warned my employee of the ex-con's preoccupation with her. Fortunately, he just stopped coming in.

(3) We took the check. There was no problem with it and they went on to spend many thousands more.

(4) I called the security number of the shopping center and after awhile they came by and escorted them from the property.

(5) I very quickly began to feel that she was responsible, but did not want to believe it. The thefts and shortages continued. I talked with her about what was happening. Finally, after several months, she was over an hour late to work. I terminated her. The thefts and shortages stopped. I felt relieved and betrayed.

(6) I told them I didn't have a corkscrew and asked them to leave. They departed. I called security. They told me that they were not supposed to get involved with in-store situations, but that they would do their best to remove them from the shopping center.

(7) I hired a new employee who by chance knew this woman socially. From then on she dealt with her whenever she came in. Her hours were scheduled partially with this in mind. She was even able to deal with sporadic bouts of attempted shoplifting (something I had never noticed) by adding the items to the bill.

Working by Mail

Regardless of how you initially meet your customers, keep a detailed record of them and their buying habits. If they are looking for something make sure you have a way to record this and to retrieve it. (One word of caution. It is often a mistake to buy something that you were not going to buy anyway just because a customer expressed an interest. Far too often you will find out that what you bought was "not quite what they had in mind" and you will be stuck with it.)

Use your mailing list to let customers know when you have new merchandise, to reacquaint them with old favorites, invite them to special functions, or to communicate with them for any other reason that serves your interest.

Consider photographs for those who are too far away to for you to conveniently meet with in person on a regular basis. If appropriate you may even expand into using a formal catalogue. The important thing is to remember to communicate with your customers both near and far.

Your list must be kept up to date. If you do not receive any business from some of your customers for a year or so they should be moved to your inactive list. Failure to periodically purge your list will make any type of direct mail effort ineffective.

This is a simplistic look at what you can do with your mailing list. If you want to expand your marketing by mail, there are many books available on the subject to give suggestions. Better than most is a book by Stan Rapp and Tom Collins called <u>The Great Marketing Turnaround</u> (ISBN 0-13-365560-1). This book is subtitled "The Age of the Individual and How to Profit from It" and that is what it is about. It contains great suggestions for creating your database (mailing list) and using it to prospect for real, money spending customers. If you are ready to kick your marketing strategy up a notch, this is the book for you.

Anyone who requests information about my beads and jewelry receives the following letter along with a current show schedule.

Lost Cities
1-800-525-3053

Thank you for your interest in Lost Cities. I've included this introduction to give you an idea of how I operate and what I have to offer.

I make several trips each year to the Himalayas, Asia, the Near East, North Africa, Indonesia, and anywhere else I can find interesting pieces. My focus-and hopefully yours-is on the old and unusual. Included in my collection are amber, Tibetan turquoise, coral, dZi and other decorated stone beads, ancient stone and glass, and a selection of antique tribal jewelry.

I conduct bead exhibition/sales in many cities throughout the country. I schedule private previews from 9 AM-8 PM for several days before each exhibition. If you would like a private preview please contact me at 1-800-525-3053 as soon as possible to arrange a convenient time. It usually takes about two hours to see everything. If you are serious about beads, this is the best way to see them. A copy of my current show schedule is enclosed.

Amber. Most of my amber is Tibetan. All of it is old. The primary characteristic of these beads is that they were made according to the forms of the raw pieces as they were found rather than molded into regular shapes. Representative photographs can be seen on page 97 of the Autumn 1992 (Volume 16, Number 1) issue of *Ornament* magazine which features an article about some of my beads.

My **turquoise** is Tibetan. The beads are hundreds of years old and have the distinctive green shading that is highly prized in the Himalayas. They vary in size from very small to several inches in diameter. Each bead is individually selected. I try to find thin flat beads with excellent color and character. The flat beads offer a much greater visible surface area by weight as compared to rounder stones. Every bead is a work of nature's art...some are pure green with no matrix, others range from thin spiderwebs to lizard-like blotches, while still others feature distinctive geometrics that seem to be painted on.

Carnelian. These too are old beads from Tibet with rich red color highlighted by blackened pitmarks from the oil and dirt of the ages. There are a variety of sizes including round and melon shapes approximately one half inch in diameter and elongated ovals ranging from one to two inches in length.

Mosaic Coral. These beads, old and Tibetan, were made by filling in the holes of irregularly shaped coral beads with a wax and pitch mixture called lakh and small pieces of coral. I think that these are some of the most exotic ethnic beads around... much nicer than the smooth polished coral beads that are significantly more expensive.

dZi and Other Decorated Agates. I usually have examples of most dZi types shown on page 216 of The History of Beads, by Lois Dubin. If you are looking for a special bead in this category, I can probably find it for you if I don't already have it. I also have a variety of the "etched carnelians" as shown on page 16 of Dubin's book.

After each trip I will send you a newsletter with representative photos and descriptions of my latest finds along with a copy of our current show schedule.

REMEMBER. The best way to see the beads is by private preview. If there is a show scheduled near you, CALL for an APPOINTMENT. If it is not possible for you to come to one of my current shows, call me anyway. I may be passing near you soon.

Sincerely,
Christina Blessing

P. S. All of the calls to my 800 number are forwarded to a voice mail box. I know that this is not as good as having someone available to take your call, but because of my travel schedule it's the only way I can make sure that you are able to contact me. I check the messages at least once a day and I will return your call promptly.

Exports

Exporting and importing are structurally similar. The differences lie in the realities of dealing with the bureaucracies of various countries. While some procedures of the U.S. Customs Service could perhaps be improved, the process of importing merchandise is reasonably straightforward... at least to your customs broker. You can usually find out what you can do and cannot do before spending a lot of time and money. The amount of money it will cost you is also possible to determine in advance. There are no bribes or special expediting charges involved.

This is not true in many foreign countries, even ones that we regard as being reasonably civilized. A letter to the editor of the *Bangkok Post* in April 1995 decried the size of the bribe (over and above customs duty) required for a friend who was moving household goods from Hong Kong to Bangkok. He had been told by his customs broker that this is the way things were done there. He was told that he should be sympathetic to the plight of the customs agents who were underpaid and needed subsidies like this (several thousand dollars) to help make ends meet. Commercial shipments can be even more intriguing. Try to make sure you understand as much as possible by checking with a broker in receiving country before making any commitments. Ask about extra costs. Start small with a partial shipment even if everything looks okay.

You will usually begin your exporting career through a contact made at a trade show or from a response to your advertising. Get the money up front unless it is a trivial sum. There is often little recourse to extract payment once your shipment has been made. Arranging for a direct wire transfer of funds into your account is the most sure way to arrange for you to get your money. (If you are going to use the incoming wire transfer of receiving payment, verify with your bank that no outgoing wire transfer can be sent from your account unless it is authorized by you in person. This seemingly unnecessary precaution will protect you from a wire fraud scam that has been making the rounds for the past few years. It seems to be especially popular with several groups from Nigeria.) Methods such as sight drafts and other means for getting paid can be explained to you by your broker or banker, if he has international experience.

When you are negotiating an overseas deal make sure it is understood who pays for what. F.O.B. warehouse, which stands for free on board at your warehouse, means the receiver is responsible for all shipping and brokerage costs. This should be your policy unless there is an overwhelming reason for you pick up some or all of the shipping cost. For example, you might agree to pay for the shipping costs involved for a small expensive package of jewelry, where the transport charges are small in comparison to the value of the goods. Still, F.O.B. is the best policy.

Probably the best method for developing export possibilities is through participation in international trade shows. The trade show promoter paves the way for customs clearance and you will have to do little more than post a customs bond (easily arranged through a customs broker) to get your samples into the country. There will also be preferred cargo expediters and brokers in attendance to help should you land any large orders. Check with these people as early as possible. Any hidden charges are part of the cost of doing business and need to be factored into the amount you charge for your merchandise.

International trade and art shows have been largely neglected by most artists and craftsmen of the US, probably because of the unfamiliarity and costs involved. While it is admittedly a gamble, it can be a very good one if you truly excel at what you do. Participating in the right international trade show could be a career making venture. If necessary, consider a co-op group effort. It could be the ticket to fame and fortune. Contact the Chamber of Commerce in Tokyo, Hong Kong, Taipei or perhaps Milan, Munich, or Paris for show information. Art periodicals with an international scope such as *Art and Auction* and *Arts of Asia* have notices of upcoming events

There are many opportunities and methods of marketing to be explored. Always keep your eyes open and ear to the ground for profitable ways to buy or sell.

Afterthought

While numerous participants in these markets have made significant sums of money starting from meager beginnings, none of the strategies discussed in this book is a get rich quick opportunity. Or even get rich slow. The greatest benefits of trading in the markets and bazaars of the world lie in doing something that is challenging, interesting, and fun to do. They offer a unique chance to take control of your time, money, and destiny.

Appendix 1
Passport Protocol

You must appear in person to get your first passport with a completed but <u>unsigned</u> passport application (DSP-11) at one of the thirteen U.S. passport agencies or at one of the several thousand post offices or federal or state courts that are authorized to accept passport applications. If you cannot find a local one in the government listings of your phone book, contact one of the regional passport agencies. If you have previously had a passport you may be able to get your next one by mail. The regional passport agencies are listed as follows:

<u>Boston Passport Agency</u>
Thomas P. O'Neill Federal Building
Room 247
10 Causeway Street
Boston, MA 02222
Information Recording 617-565-6990
Inquiries 617-565-6990

<u>Chicago Passport Agency</u>
Kluczynski Federal Building
Suite 380
230 South Dearborn Street
Chicago, IL 60604
Information Recording 312-353-7155
Inquiries 312-734-8193

Honolulu Passport Agency
New Federal Building
Room C-106
300 Ala Moana Boulevard
Honolulu, HI 96850
Information Recording 808-522-8283

Houston Passport Agency
Mickey Leland Federal Building
Suite 1100
1919 Smith
Houston, TX 77002
Information Recording 713-653-3153

Los Angeles Passport Agency
11000 Wilshire Boulevard
Los Angeles, CA 90024
Information Recording 310-235-7070

Miami Passport Agency
Federal Office Building
3rd Floor
61 Southwest First Avenue
Miami, FL 33130
Information Recording 305-536-5395

New Orleans Passport Agency
Postal Services Building
Room T-12005
701 Loyola Avenue
New Orleans, LA 70013
Information Recording 504-589-6728
Inquiries 504-589-6161

Philadelphia Passport Agency
U.S. Customs House
Room 103
200 Chestnut Street
Philadelphia, PA 19106
Information Recording 215-597-7482
Inquiries 215-597-7480

San Francisco Passport Agency
Tishman Speyer Building
Suite 300
525 Market
San Francisco, CA 94105
Inquiries 415-744-7569

Seattle Passport Agency
Federal Office Building
Room 992
915 Second Avenue
Seattle, WA 98174
Information Recording 206-220-7788

Stamford Passport Agency
One Landmark Square
Broad and Atlantic Streets
Stamford, CT 06901
Information Recording 203-325-4401
Inquiries 203-325-3530

Washington, D.C. Passport Agency
1425 K Street, N.W.
Washington, D.C. 20524
Information Recording 202-647-0518

In addition to your completed, unsigned passport application, you also need proof of U.S. citizenship, proof of identity, photographs, and the correct fee.

The following methods of proving U.S. citizenship are listed in order of preference. Each step further down the line you have to go, the more delays and other difficulties you can expect.

First, you can use a previously issued passport. Obviously, if you have never had one before you will need to submit other evidence of citizenship.

If you were born in the United States you can use a certified copy of your birth certificate. The birth record must have been filed shortly after birth and must be certified with the registrar's signature and official seal. A certified copy can be obtained from the Bureau of Vital Statistics in the city, state, county, or territory where you were born. A birth certificate that was filed more than one year from the date of birth may be acceptable if you can show a plausible reason for the creation of the record.

If you cannot obtain a birth certificate the road may become a bit rocky. Get a notice from a state registrar that no birth record exists, accompanied by the best secondary evidence you can find. This might include a baptismal certificate, a hospital birth record, affidavits of people who have personal knowledge of the facts of your birth, or other evidence such as school records, family Bible records, or newspaper files. A personal knowledge affidavit should be backed up by at least one public record showing that you were born in the U.S.

If you were born outside the United States you can use a Certificate of Naturalization, a Certificate of Citizenship, a Report of Birth Abroad of a Citizen of the United States (Form FS-240), or a Certification of Birth (Form

If you are a U.S. citizen but have none of these documents, take your best evidence and story to the nearest passport office and throw yourself at their mercy. They may be able to help but it will take time, probably quite a bit of time.

You now need to offer proof that you are who you say you are. The person accepting your application is the one you have to convince. The following four types of identification are the only ones that pull any weight and then only if they have your signature and readily identify you by physical description or photograph. They include a previous U.S. passport, a certificate of naturalization or citizenship, a valid driver's license, or a valid government identification card. A social security card, credit card, expired documents, and other things that you thought might work will not be acceptable.

If you cannot show one of the four pieces of acceptable identification, you need to bring someone with you who is a U.S. citizen or permanent resident alien who has known you for at least two years. This person must sign an affidavit in the presence of the person who executes your passport application. The witness will be required to establish his own identity. You will also need to show them whatever other type of identification you happen to have. Good luck.

You also need to furnish two recent identical 2" x 2" photographs of yourself. They will probably need to be taken by one of the passport photography professionals as the passport agency will not accept the reasonably priced ones available through vending machines. Call around to check prices. You might be able to save yourself some money. Sometimes there are price wars in this highly profitable business. Once in Houston the price dropped at two warring competitors outside the passport office from around five dollars per photo to one dollar. In situations like this or when you find them reasonably priced overseas, get a dozen or more to use with your future visa applications. In fact once you have decided to get them, make sure to get at least enough to handle your current visa needs. No dark glasses, no hat, no head coverings unless they are worn for religious reasons.

The fee for a ten year passport is $65 ($55 plus $10 appearance fee if you apply in person) at the time of this writing. It can be paid by check, bank draft, or money order. You can also pay by cash at a passport agency. Legal tender laws not withstanding, cash is not accepted by all post offices or clerks of court.

Request a large 48 page passport at the time you apply. There is no extra charge and getting one will save you another trip if you travel a lot to places that require visas. Alas, for reasons unknown the 48 page passports are not always in stock. If you need more pages added you can trek back to the passport office or get them at an embassy or consulate overseas.

You can apply for your passport by mail only if all of the following are true:

(1) You have been issued a passport within 12 years prior to your new application.

(2) You are able to submit your most recent U.S. passport with your new application.

(3) Your previous passport was issued on or after your 16th birthday.

(4) You use the same name as that on your most recent

passport or you have had your name changed by marriage or court order.

If all of the above is in order contact one of the regional passport agencies listed above to obtain an Application for Passport by Mail (Form DSP-82). You may be able to get one from your travel agent. Proceed as follows:

(1) Complete, sign, and date the application.

(2) Include the date of your departure if your schedule is tight. This may speed things up somewhat. Otherwise it will usually take several weeks for processing.

(3) Enclose your previous passport.

(4) Enclose two identical 2" x 2" photographs as described above.

(5) Enclose the $55 passport fee. (You get a $10 discount if you are eligible to apply by mail.) Make sure to verify that this figure is correct. Checks, bank drafts, cashier's checks, or money orders are all acceptable. No cash by mail.

(6) If your name has changed, submit the original or certified copy of the court order or marriage certificate that shows the change of name.

(7) Mail the completed application to one of the regional passport agencies.

Appendix 2
Embassies and Consulates

Afghanistan
202-234-3770

Algeria
202-265-2800

Argentina
202-939-6400
FL 305-373-1889
NY 212-603-0415
TX 713-871-8935

Armenia
202-387-8327

Australia
CA 213-469-4300
CA 415-362-6160
HI 808-524-5050
NY 212-408-8400
TX 713-629-9131

Austria
202-895-6767
CA 310-444-9310
IL 312-222-1515

Bahamas
202-319-2660

Bangladesh
202-342-8373

Belarus
202-986-1604

Belgium
202-333-6900
CA 213-857-1244
GA 404-659-2150
IL 312-263-6624
NY 212-586-5110

Belize
202-332-9636
NY 212-599-0233

Bhutan
212-826-1919

Bolivia
202-232-4828
202-483-4410
CA 415-495-5173
NY 212-687-0530

Botswana
202-244-4490
CA 213-626-8484

Brazil
202-745-2828
CA 213-651-2664
FL 305-285-6200
IL 312-464-0244
NY 212-757-3080

Bulgaria
202-387-7969

Burkina Faso
202-332-5577

Burma (Myanmar)
202-332-9044

Cameroon
202-265-8790

Canada
202-682-1740

Chile
202-785-3159
CA 310-785-0113
CA 415-982-7662
FL 305-373-8623
NY 212-980-3366

China
202-328-2517
IL 312-803-0095
TX 713-524-4311
CA 213-380-2506
NY 212-330-7409

Colombia
202-332-7476
GA 404-237-1045
IL 312-341-0658
MA 617-536-6222
MN 612-933-2408
TX 713-527-8919

Congo
202-726-5500

Costa Rica
202-328-6628
CA 415-392-8488
FL 305-377-4242
IL 312-263-2772
NY 212-425-2620

Cuba
202-797-8609
U.S. citizens may need a Treasury Department license to engage in any transactions related to Cuba. For information contact:

Licensing Division Office
Office of Foreign Assets Control
Department of the Treasury
1331 G Street NW
Washington,D.C. 20220
202-622-2480

Cyprus
202-462-5772

Czech Republic
202-363-6315

Denmark
202-234-4300
CA 310-443-2090
NY 212-223-4545

Djbouti
202-331-0270

Dominica
212-599-8478

Dominican Republic
202-332-6280
CA 415-982-5144
FL 305-358-3221
IL 312-772-6363
NY 212-768-2480

Ecuador
202-234-7166
CA 213-628-3014
FL 305-539-8214
IL 312-329-0266
MA 617-523-2700

Egypt
NY 212-759-7120
CA 415-346-9700
IL 312-828-9162
TX 713-961-4915

El Salvador
202-331-4032
CA 213-383-5776
CA 415-781-7924
FL 305-371-8850
NY 212-889-3608
TX 713-270-6239

Eritrea
202-429-1991

Estonia
212-247-1450

Ethiopia
202-234-2282

Finland
202-363-2430
CA 310-203-9903
NY 212-75-4400

France
202-944-6200
CA 310-479-4426
CA 415-397-4330
FL 305-372-9798
GA 404-522-4226
HI 808-599-4458
IL 312-787-5359
TX 713-528-2181
Includes information for French Polynesia,
French Guiana, etc.

Gambia
202-785-1399

Republic of Georgia
202-393-6060

Germany
202-298-4000
CA 415-775-1061
NY 212-308-8700
TX 713-627-7770

Ghana
202-686-4520

Greece
202-939-5818

CA 310-826-5555
CA 415-775-2102
LA 504-523-1167
NY 212-988-5500
TX 713-840-7522

Grenada
202-265-2561

Guatemala
202-745-4952
CA 415-788-5651
NY 212-686-3837
TX 713-953-9531

Haiti
202-332-4090
FL 305-859-2003

Honduras
202-223-0185
CA 213-383-9244
FL 305-447-8927
TX 713-622-4572

Hong Kong
The transfer of control of Hong Kong from Great Britain to China in 1997 will undoubtedly result in a variety of changes, many of which will only become evident after the passage of time. Check your plans with the Chinese embassy or consulate.

Hungary
202-362-6730

Iceland
202-265-6653

India
202-939-9839
CA 415-668-0683
IL 312-781-6280
NY 212-879-7800

Indonesia
202-775-5200
CA 213-383-5126
CA 415-474-9571
NY 212-879-0600

Ireland
202-462-3939
CA 415-392-4214
IL 312-337-1868
NY 212-319-2555

Israel
202-364-5500
CA 213-651-5700
IL 312-565-3300

Italy
202-328-5500
CA 310-820-0622
CA 415-931-4924
FL 305-374-6322
IL 312-467-1550
LA 504-524-2272
MA 617-542-0484
MI 313-963-8560
NJ 201-643-1448
PA 215-592-7329

Jamaica
202-452-0660
IL 312-663-0023

Japan
202-939-6800
AK 907-279-8428
CA 213-624-8305
CA 415-777-3533
FL 305-530-9090
GA 404-892-2700
IL 312-280-0400
LA 504-529-2101
MO 816-471-0111
NY 212-371-8222
OR 503-221-1811
TX 713-652-2977
WA 206-682-9107

Jordan
202-966-2664

Kazakhstan
202-333-4504

Kenya
202-387-6101

North Korea
    U.S. citizens may need a license to engage in any transactions related to North Korea. For information contact:
Licensing Division Office
Office of Foreign Assets Control
Department of the Treasury
1311 G Street N.W.
Washington, D.C. 20220
202-622-2480

South Korea
202-939-5660
CA 213-385-9300
CA 415-921-2251
GA 404-522-1611
HI 808-595-6109
TX 713-961-0186
WA 206-441-1011

Kyrgyz Republic
202-628-0433

Laos
202-332-6416

Latvia
202-726-8213

Lebanon
202-939-6300
Possible red tape.

Lesotho
202-797-5533

Liberia
202-723-0437

Libya
Don't even think about it.

Lithuania
202-234-5860

Luxembourg
202-265-4171

CA 415-788-0816
FL 305-373-1300
NY 212-888-6664

Madagascar
202-265-5525
CA 800-856-2721
NY 212-986-9841

Malawi
202-797-1007
Strict dress codes.

Malaysia
202-328-2700
CA 213-621-2991
NY 212-490-2722

Maldives
212-599-6195

Mali
202-332-2249

Malta
202-462-3611
MA 617-259-1391
NY 212-725-2345
TX 713-497-2100

Mauritania
202-232-5700

Mauritius
202-244-1491

Mexico
202-736-1000
CA 213-351-6800
CA 619-231-8414
CO 303-830-6702
IL 312-855-1380
LA 504-522-3596
NY 212-689-0456
TX 713-463-9426
TX 512-227-9145

Mongolia
202-333-7117

Morocco
202-462-7979
NY 212-213-9644

Mozambique
202-293-7146

Namibia
202-986-0540

Nepal
202-667-4550
NY 212-370-4188

Netherlands
202-244-5300
IL 312-856-0110
NY 212-246-1429
TX 713-622-8000

Netherland Antilles
202-244-5300

New Zealand
202-328-4800

Nicaragua
202-939-6531

Niger
202-483-4224

Nigeria
202-822-1500
Be very careful.

Norway
202-333-6000
CA 415-986-0766
CA 213-933-7717
MN 612-332-3338
NY 212-421-7333
TX 713-521-2900

Oman
202-387-1980

Pakistan
202-939-6295
NY 212-879-5800

Panama
202-483-1407

Papua New Guinea
202-745-3680

Paraguay
202-483-6960

Peru
202-833-9860
CA 213-383-9896
CA 415-362-5185
FL 305-374-1407
IL 312-853-6173
TX 713-781-5000

Philippines
202-467-9300
CA 213-387-5321
CA 415-433-6666
HI 808-595-6316
NY 212-764-1330

Poland
202-232-4517
NY 212-889-8360

Portugal
202-332-3007
CA 415-346-3400
MA 617-536-8740
NJ 201-622-7300
NY 212-246-4580
RI 401-272-2003

Romania
202-232-4747
NY 212-682-9120

Russia
202-939-8907
CA 415-202-9800
WA 206-728-1910

Singapore
202-537-3100

Slovak Republic
202-965-5164

South Africa
202-966-1650
CA 310-657-9200
IL 312-939-7929
NY 212-213-4880

Spain
202-452-0100
CA 415-922-2995
FL 305-446-5511
NY 212-355-4080
TX 713-783-6200

Sri Lanka
202-483-4025
NJ 201-627-7855
NY 212-986-7040

Sudan
202-338-8565

Suriname
202-244-7488

Swaziland
202-362-6683

Sweden
202-467-2600
NY 212-751-5900

Switzerland
202-745-7900
CA 310-575-1145
CA 415-788-2272
GA 404-870-2000
IL 312-915-0061
NY 212-758-2560
TX 713-650-0000

Syria
202-232-6313

Taiwan
202-895-1800

Tanzania
202-939-6125

Thailand
202-944-3600
CA 213-937-1894
IL 312-236-2447
NY 212-754-1770

Tunisia
202-862-1850
CA 415-922-9222
NY 212-272-6962

Turkey
202-659-0742
IL 312-263-0644
NY 212-949-0160
TX 713-622-5849

Ukraine
202-333-7507

United Kingdom
202-986-0205
CA 310-477-3322
GA 404-524-5856
IL 312-346-1810
OH 216-621-7674

Uruguay
202-331-1313
CA 213-394-5777
FL 305-443-9764
NY 212-753-8191

Uzbekistan
212-486-7570

Venezuela
202-342-2214
CA 415-512-8340
FL 305-577-3834
IL 312-236-9655
NY 212-826-1660
TX 713-961-5141

Vietnam
212-679-3779

British Virgin Islands
202-986-0205

British West Indies
202-986-0205

French West Indies
202-944-6200

Yemen
202-965-4760

Zaire
202-234-7690

Zambia
202-265-9717

Zimbabwe
202-332-7100

Appendix 3
Customs Brokers, Customs Offices, and Fish and Wildlife

NEW YORK

Customs Brokers

Advance Shipping Co.
(Special Guidance for the New Importer)
212-964-1050
212-964-1059 Fax

Hudson Shipping
(Specializing in Fine Art and Antiques)
212-487-2600
718-276-5302
718-656-6226

Jet Air Service Inc.
JFK International
718-656-7430

U.S. Customs (New York)
800-697-3662

Fish and Wildlife (New York)
718-482-4922

MIAMI

Customs Brokers

Emery Customs Brokers
305-591-9250

J P Reynolds Company
305-592-9916
305-592-9948 Fax

MSAS Customs Logistics Inc.
305-591-8740

U.S. Customs (Miami)
305-860-2800

Fish and Wildlife (Miami)
305-871-5015

HOUSTON

Customs Brokers

Emery Customs Brokers
713-590-5482

R W Smith and Co.
713-590-5959

Ghedi International
713-443-7400

U.S. Customs (Houston)
713-671-1062

Fish and Wildlife (Houston)
713-229-2559

DALLAS

Customs Brokers

Emery Customs Brokers
817-481-6755

DFW International Services
214-641-1218

Harper Group
214-456-0730

U.S.Customs (Dallas)
214-574-2170

Fish and Wildlife (Dallas)
214-574-3254

CHICAGO

Customs Brokers

Robinson
708-699-8220

Emery Worldwide
708-766-9137

Kintetsu International USA
708-595-8885

U.S. Customs (Chicago)
312-353-6150

Fish and Wildlife (Chicago)
708-298-3250

LOS ANGELES

Customs Brokers

Dukes Clearance Corporation
310-645-4001

Emery Worldwide
310-670-1007
310-642-0503 Fax

U.S. Customs (Los Angeles)
310-514-6030

Fish and Wildlife (Los Angeles)
310-297-0062

SAN FRANCISCO

Customs Brokers

Emery Customs Brokers
415-873-7580

Hoyt Shepston
415-952-6930

U.S. Customs (San Francisco)
415-744-7569

Fish & Wildlife (San Francisco)
510-792-0222

SEATTLE

Customs Brokers

Tower Group International
206-623-2593 (Ocean)
206-251-9700 (Air)

Emery
206-433-5064

Novanco
206-872-7757

U.S. Customs (Seattle)
206-553-4676

Fish & Wildlife (Seattle)
360-902-2200

Reading and Research

The Airline Passenger's Guerrilla Handbook, by George Albert Brown (ISBN 0-924022-04-03) covers everything in and around airports and airplanes. Many useful hints and suggestions.

The World Atlas of Food, edited by Gloria Hale (ISBN 0-671-07211-0), is a guide to regional cooking around the world. Each chapter begins with a section that gives you an overall idea of what they're eating and drinking in that region. The recipes that follow tell you exactly what is in it. This comprehensive resource will keep you from having to buy a separate cookbook for each of your destinations.

Import/Export , by Dr. Carl A. Nelson (ISBN 9-8306-4052-5) has detailed information on international finance (letters of credit, sight drafts, etc.) and a somewhat formal explanation of the forms, rules, and regulations of the import/export process. Much of what is covered will be handled by your broker or shipper. However, if you are arranging large shipments or like to know how things work from the inside you may find some answers here.

The Art Dealers, by Alan Jones and Laura de Coppet (ISBN 0-517-55302-3) is subtitled "The Powers Behind the Scene Tell How the Art World Works". This is a collection of over thirty candid interviews with influential art dealers about the business of art.

How to Make the Most of Your Investments in Antiques and Collectibles, by Harry Rinker (ISBN 0-87795-933-1) styles itself as "The First Insider's Guide to Manipulating the Antiques and Collectibles Markets to Maximize Your Investment". It both provokes and answers questions about what is going on out there.

Every time I read the "From the Notebooks" section of Bruce Chatwin's The Songlines (ISBN 0-670-80605-6), I long to travel somewhere wonderful and exotic.

If you find yourself thinking about buying your own building, Real Estate Quick and Easy, by Roy T. Maloney (ISBN 0-913527-00-1) gives you a lot to consider. It's a fun read, full of practical tips and philosophical musings.

Exhibit Marketing, by Edward A. Chapman, Jr. (ISBN 0-07-010669-X) takes you step by step through the planning, set-up, operation, and evaluation of your exhibit. Detailed suggestions and checklists.

Books by futurists such as Alvin Toffler, John Naisbitt, and Faith Popcorn provide thoughtful material about where we may be heading. Their views of macro trends may have implications for your micro business.

How to Make $20,000 in Antiques and Collectibles Without Leaving Your Job, by Bruce E. Johnson (ISBN 0-345-34624-6) covers garage and yard sales, flea markets, local auctions, and antique malls. The final section of the book discusses different services that you may be able to offer to the antique and collectible community. Included are listings of a wide range of related organizations and publications.

Influencing With Integrity, by Genie Z. Laborde (ISBN 0-9613172-0-5) takes a comprehensive, ethical look at the application of Neuro-Linguistic Programming to the solution of business problems. It discusses strategies for reading the intentions of others and swaying their opinions.

The Complete Collector's Guide to Fakes and Forgeries, by Colin Haynes (ISBN 0-87069-512-6) chronicles the history of reproductions and misrepresentations in art, jewelry, antiques, and collectibles. The techniques and ingenuity used by these crooks will astound you. It may also make you afraid to buy anything for awhile.

The Silk Road, by Irene M. Franck and David M. Brown-stone (ISBN 0-8160-1122-2) is the story of the trading route from Europe to China through Central Asia made famous by Marco Polo. It tells the tales of warriors, adventurers, and kings, and most importantly the merchants and traders who were its lifeblood.

Bottom-Up Marketing, by Al Ries and Jack Trout (ISBN 0-07-052733-4) is a detailed study of tactic based marketing strategy. It uses the successful and unsuccessful marketing campaigns of Fortune 500 companies as examples. The virtues of narrow focus are extolled.

The Great Marketing Turnaround, by Stan Rapp and Tom Collins (ISBN 0-13-365560-1) explores the shift from generalized mass marketing to individually targeted direct marketing. It discusses innovative ways for building, expanding, and profiting from your database (mailing list). There are many inspirational examples that cover the range from micro-sized businesses to multinational giants.

Travel Books. Fodor's, Lonely Planet, and Impact Guides all have something special to offer the traveler.

I have been pleased with Fodor's quality hotel and restaurant recommendations. Their guides also provide good historical and background information.

Lonely Planet's guides provide maps of areas that are not covered by other travel books. They also contain practical advice for dealing with bureaucratic problems and life on the streets.

Impact Guides have detailed information on shopping areas and some first rate dining suggestions.

Index

Treasures from the World's Bazaars

My search for the old and unusual continues. I specialize in Tibetan turquoise, coral, amber, and agate beads from the Himalayas, but I also have a large collection of ancient and antique stone and glass beads form other parts of the world. Most of these beads are sold as components to jewelry artists and designers, but some finished pieces are available. I conduct public and private showings of my discoveries in cities coast to coast including New York, Boston, Philadelphia, Chicago, Houston, Santa Fe, Scottsdale, San Diego, Los Angeles, San Francisco, Portland, and Seattle. To receive a show schedule or arrange an appointment in any of these cities, CALL 800-525-3053 or write to me at:

Lost Cities
3395 South Jones #204
Las Vegas, NV 89102

If you need help on a project that involves old beads, weavings or ethnographic items, leave a brief message on 800-525-3053 or send a description to me at the above address. I'll let you know if I can assist you as a supplier or on a fee basis.